ANGEL OF DEATH

UNCOVER THE DARKNESS OF NIGHTMARE NURSE, JANE TOPPAN

RYAN GREEN

For Helen, Harvey, Frankie and Dougie

Disclaimer

This book is about real people committing real crimes. The story has been constructed by facts but some of the scenes, dialogue and characters have been fictionalised.

Polite Note to the Reader

This book is written in British English except where fidelity to other languages or accents are appropriate. Some words and phrases may differ from US English.

Copyright © Ryan Green 2024

All rights reserved

ISBN: 9798301850745

YOUR FREE BOOK IS WAITING

From bestselling author Ryan Green

There is a man who is officially classed as **"Britain's most dangerous prisoner"**

The man's name is Robert Maudsley, and his crimes earned him the nickname **"Hannibal the Cannibal"**

This free book is an exploration of his story...

amazonkindle nook kobo iBooks

★★★★★ *"Ryan brings the horrifying details to life. I can't wait to read more by this author!"*

Get a free copy of **Robert Maudsley: Hannibal the Cannibal** when you sign up to join my Reader's Group.

www.ryangreenbooks.com/free-book

CONTENTS

Medical Mysteries 7
Luck of the Irish 14
Service and Virtue 24
Jolly Jane 38
House Bound 53
Return of the Cuckoo 67
Family Curse 83
Clipping the Angel's Wings 100
A Legacy of Carnage 112
Want More? 124
Every Review Helps 125
About Ryan Green 126
More Books by Ryan Green 127
Free True Crime Audiobook 132

Medical Mysteries

There was something wrong with the charts or there was something wrong with their diagnosis. Something was not adding up.

Dilated pupils, photophobia, hallucinatory rambling. This particular constellation of symptoms would not typically be expected with the infection that the patient was being treated for. And the fever? The patient was hot to the touch, hot enough to fry an egg on by the account of one nurse, yet there wasn't a drop of sweat anywhere on her body. Simply put, this patient's clinical presentation didn't make the slightest bit of sense, at least not until the old woman's eyes gave out prompting a long-buried clinical pearl to spring to the forefront of the doctor's mind.

"Hot as a hare, blind as a bat, dry as a bone, red as a beet, mad as a hatter." The old mnemonic from medical school that they had often recited in a sing-song cadence. Every one of the patient's new symptoms could be explained away by atropine poisoning, save for one. There was no hammering heart. If anything, the patient's heart rate was dangerously low. The low heart rate was completely contrary to the typical presentation of atropine poisoning. Besides, it took only a cursory glance at the patient's charts to see that there was no atropine being administered to the patient at all. While the administration of atropine might be considered should her heart rate drop any further, at this point in time they wanted her to pass whatever infected material was in her body, not trap it inside with a medication that had well-documented anti-diarrhoeal effects.

So, the doctors returned to the drawing board, and the family was none the wiser about their dear grandmother's rapid circling of the drain. Without sweat, her body temperature continued to rise with the fever, her brain began to cook. It was a race against time to solve the mystery of her condition. The task of prolonging that race fell to the nursing staff.

Carrying the old woman in a makeshift hammock of her bedsheets strung between the sturdiest of them, they took her down to the baths and settled her into the iced water in an effort to bring her temperature down. The shock of the sudden change in temperature could easily have given her a heart attack, but her heart continued to beat just as slow and steady as if she were sitting out on her porch enjoying a summers evening. The complete lack of cardiac reactivity to the ice baths only served to draw more confusion and beard-stroking from the cadre of doctors who, by now, were far more invested in the solving of their intriguing puzzle than in saving an old woman's life.

The infection explained the rising fever, the reddening of the skin could be due to the infection having passed into the bloodstream. From the blood, the infection could rapidly spread to the eyes and brain explaining some of the patient's symptoms, but if her blood were carrying a contagion throughout her body, surely there would have been more dramatic and possibly even potentially lethal signs of it by now. And what about the inexplicable halting of saliva, sweat and all other mucus production? If this were a simple bacterial infection, then how could it be producing so many different effects without any of their usual connotations?

Most puzzling of all remained the heart. It should have been hammering away as the body fought back against the infection.

The fever alone should have set it into a frenzy, and the sudden ice dunk should have made it beat so fast as to be practically jumping from her sunken chest, yet there was nothing. It was completely contradictory to both the original diagnosis and the unspoken hypothesis shared among the doctors that some careless or incompetent nurse had accidentally injected atropine instead of the prescribed morphine that was intended to keep the old dear comfortable while she recovered.

They had no choice but to go back to basics. If they assumed that all of her symptoms were a coherent expression of a single illness, what would it be?

There were certain viral fevers that had the potential to provoke similar symptoms, at least going by second-hand accounts. The problem with that idea was that such fevers were typically too exotic to find their way to an elderly woman who hadn't left her hometown of Boston for more than a decade and had a social life about as active as she was currently, laid up in a hospital bed. The ultimate detractor, however, was that none of these viral fevers were consistent with the patient's lowered heart rate.

Bacterial pneumonia and appendicitis were both ruled out as swiftly as septicaemia. If it were any of these, there would have been specific signs that their testing could identify, even if the patient was generally asymptomatic. A kidney infection had been the original diagnosis and seemed likely given the blood that had been present in the patient's urine, but that had subsided now.

The final suggestion, put forth by one of the younger doctors and reviled by all the others was that she had perhaps indulged in too many drugs of leisure, dosing herself with some cocktail of medications to ease her pain or her boredom prior to hospitalisation that were now interacting poorly with what the nurses were administering.

None of the upstanding doctors knew of any abuse of restricted substances, of course, nor could they countenance an upstanding woman of their generation having indulged in such nonsense. Testing of the blood that had been drawn from her had shown no irregularities that one might associate with the misuse of chemicals, so they were driven by their own preconceived notions back to the drawing board once more.

Meanwhile, the nurses continued to care for the old woman as though she were their own mother, lavishing time and attention on her that they could scarcely spare, given how busy the ward was. Dear kindly Jane even sat after her shift was done and held the woman's hand as she drifted in and out of consciousness just so the poor woman wouldn't be scared and alone.

The nurse ended up drifting to sleep with her head laid upon the patient, much to the doctor's initial dismay, but then they realised the significance of it. Nobody could have tolerated laying their head upon the patient prior to now. A quick check showed that her temperature was dropping again. Whatever had caused the mysterious symptoms seemed to have passed away as surely as it had arrived. The old woman's eyes opened and the doctors could plainly see that the vast black expanse of her formerly dilated pupils had shrunk back down to a normal size. She could see again, speak again, make some degree of sense, even if the fever had cooked her brain enough to ostensibly call her lucidity into question. The puzzling array of signs and symptoms, as mysterious as they'd been, now morphed back into what could reasonably be expected of a kidney infection that was being treated. Her heart, the mystery at the centre of everything, was back to beating a steady staccato rhythm.

For most of the doctors, that was the end. There were always too many patients and too many mysteries to let one that had solved itself weigh on them. In many ways, the human body was still a mystery, and the ways that it behaved when put under duress were equally mysterious. The woman, now scarcely more sapient than the bed she was laid out on, was old. Age brought with it a plethora of slow decay and a cornucopia of mishaps and malfunctions, some inexplicable, some absurdly paradoxical.

Sometimes systems failed when they should have worked perfectly, sometimes systems worked perfectly when wear and tear should have dictated their failure long ago. In a machine as complex and enigmatic as the human body, things just went haywire once in a while, and the physician's job became less about rooting out the cause and more about keeping the symptoms at bay until the machinery sorted itself out and started turning over the way that it was meant to again.

To the few that still entertained theories, their minds had all gone to the slow build-up of poisons in a system. The madness of a hatter has been attributed to felting chemicals, particularly mercury. Similarly, heavy metals like lead, mercury or arsenic, all common in this era, had the ability to prevent messages from travelling from the brain to the sweat glands, resulting in anhidrosis, the inability to sweat. If you considered the span of an entire lifetime of potential exposures, there were plenty of opportunities for this mystery to be solved.

Then it began all over again. Just as it seemed that the old woman had somehow beaten her infection, her heart began to slow and her respiration shallowed. Each breath that she took was a dry whisper, and the heat began to rise once more. It wasn't so dramatic this time. There were no frantic rushes to dunk her in ice or the like, just the nurse by her bedside dabbing at her with cold water and cooing over her when she showed the faintest sign of awareness. And most terrible of all was that this sudden change of course would, in some sad way, have been a relief. If somehow she had survived the infection that was clearly meant to take her life and managed to claw herself back to some semblance of health, there would be no leaving the hospital for her. She would require care for the rest of her life, which would be immensely costly for everyone involved, and with nobody to advocate for her and no money to speak of, she most likely would have been quietly discharged to roam the streets, mindless and desolate until some other sickness or accident took her. If anything, it would be a kindness now for the sickness to finish her off. An act of long-delayed mercy by God.

When her breathing grew more shallow and her heart began to slow ever more, there was no questioning it this time around. It had lost all element of surprise. This was death, inevitable and kind. The same nurse who'd cared for her through the last crisis was back again, dabbing at her face with cold water, doing all that she could to make the journey to the next world more comfortable for her, but there was nothing more aggressive to be done. In the early hours of the morning, she passed away in such absolute silence that nobody even knew that she was dead until it was over.

It was another clue in the mystery if any of the doctors had still been interested enough to try and solve it. That silence. The absence of a death rattle. It would have supported their suspicions about atropine poisoning.

Examination of the body after death would have uncovered that the inflammation of the kidneys that characterised the infection had entirely receded, that the brain damage from the peak fever was considerably less widespread than would have been expected and that there was not, in fact, any good reason that the woman should have died at all. She was weak frail and elderly, but beyond that, there was no systemic breakdown or organ failure that might have explained her death. A clever medical examiner might have worked out that she had died from asphyxiation, but that there had been no signs of smothering. A very clever one, with access to blood tests that wouldn't become available for decades, would have been able to identify the cocktail of morphine and atropine being pumped around the woman's system as the primary cause of her death, with the morphine having weakened her breathing to the point where she could no longer survive. As for the inexplicable lowering of the heart rate, if they had access to studies that wouldn't be published for a few more years, they would know that in low doses, atropine has the opposite effect to when a patient receives a full dose. If they're receiving tiny but regular injections of atropine alongside their other medication, then it could quite easily have built up into both the observed symptoms from the crisis and the eventual cause of death.

This clever doctor, with foreknowledge of future advancements in medicine, could then have checked the supplies of both the drugs indicated, to determine whether they had been used in an inappropriate manner, despite the tiny doses being taken to cover up any theft. From there it would have been a simple enough matter to narrow down the potential culprits to the nurses working on the ward, and from there to pinpoint Jane, who had been so attentive to the victim in her dying hours.

Of course, no such doctor existed. Nor was any posthumous examination of the body ever made. If a doctor heard hoofbeats, they were beholden by logic to believe that they were dealing with horses, not zebras. The simplest answer was not some concoction of drugs being illicitly injected into the elderly, but simply that an old woman had succumbed to her illness. And so it went. One elderly patient after another dropped dead on the ward, and not a single eyebrow raised. One after another after another.

Luck of the Irish

Peter and Bridget Kelley wed in Ireland before immigrating to America to start their new lives together in the late 1840s. They were young, stupid and fully expected that they'd arrive at Ellis Island to be handed a pot of gold and some acres of land to call their own. Perhaps naïve is a better word than stupid, though in Peter's case a less accurate one. They found their way to Boston where they were soon directed to an almost entirely Irish neighbourhood where they were finally able to rent a room, and the two set out to find whatever work they could to support themselves until the inevitable good fortune that they'd been promised in America had a chance to catch up to them.

Neither of them had any marketable skills beyond those they'd learned living in the countryside of Ireland, but as it turned out in the new world just being able to keep house was enough to earn you a steady wage. Bridget took up work in a laundry, while Peter somehow convinced people that he was a competent enough man with a needle and thread to do piecemeal work for the burgeoning garment industry. In those days clothing was not mass-produced and assembled in a single factory, but an order for clothing would be taken by a tailor along with all the necessary measurements. The various pieces of cloth were cut to measure by one person, then sent along to the next who would do the seaming, then along to the next to do the buttons and so forth until each item found its way back to the tailor that had taken the job. The tailor then bore the burden of paying everyone the item of clothing had gone to along the way their meagre pittance for doing his entire job for him. With Bridget working laundries, it was actually relatively easy for Peter to pick up extra work too, restitching and repairing clothes as needed when they came in damaged. He worked himself day and night to try and provide for his ever-growing family.

Their first daughter Nellie Kelley was born in 1850, Delia in '52 and Honora last in '54. The Kelleys moved from a single room in a shared house to an apartment of their own, one with only a pair of bedrooms for the five of them, but still far larger than anything they'd ever had before. Peter's obsessive work became all the more necessary to keep them afloat. He was in competition with every new immigrant arriving in Boston, and a good portion of them actually knew how to sew before they'd started work, not to mention being willing to work for a fraction of what he needed for each job to keep his kids afloat. Bridget had stopped work to raise the kids, but as they grew older the newly passed mandatory education law meant that Nellie was out of the house, with Delia soon to follow. Only Honora was left over, to trail along at her mother's heels in the laundries when Bridget went back to work. Getting underfoot, getting backhanded, and getting scolded for merely existing.

She was far from the only child there, and the owners didn't care so long as the mothers got on with their work, but it was hardly the most stimulating environment for what was proving to be a fairly bright child. Surrounded by clouds of steam and noxious chemicals all day long, it was more surprising that she didn't succumb to her natural curiosity and end up dead than that, on occasion, she went wandering out of sight among the vats.

Meanwhile, the pressure was beginning to mount on Peter. He was doing all he could to make ends meet, taking on more and more work wherever he could find it, but there weren't enough hours in the day to do it all. He fell behind on orders which delayed garment production and his reputation as reliable, the only thing that the man really had going for him despite all his time in the industry, soon began to crumble.

His stitch work seemed to be getting worse with every passing day too. Between exhaustion and the strain, his hands had begun to shake and tremor. The only time that they seemed to still was when he had a drink in him. American-made bourbon whiskey was his drink of choice, contrary to all expectations of an Irishman, but he drank it like there was no tomorrow coming and like someone else was footing the bill. He needed it, to steady him, to get him through all he had to do, to make it so the three lovely little girls he had at home didn't feel so much like anchors strung around his neck, dragging him down into the mire.

Alcohol may have been a plaster over the wound in his psyche, but it was a short-lived solution that ultimately exacerbated all of his problems. If he was a bad stitcher sober, one can only imagine how shoddy his work got when he was drunk, or worse yet, hungover. The mornings he'd once used to diligently clear his orders were now spent laid up in bed. The evenings he'd once spent working late were now dedicated to the sole purpose of drinking away all his worries. In the afternoon he would work, because he had to, but it now lacked a sense of accomplishment or urgency. It was more like work had become just another excruciating step in a staggering line of insufferable steps that he had to climb to get back to the pub.

The only salvation for the family was their mother. Bridget lived up to her name as a goddess of hearth and home, keeping the family together, caring for them with the meagre means available and shielding the children from the worst excesses of their father.

Some men become angry or violent when they turn to drink, but Peter got strange. He was maudlin at the best of times, but with a few drinks in him, he went from merely depressed and off the slippery slope into bizarre. Looking at him through a modern lens, it seems likely that he suffered from some mild form of schizophrenia that he usually consciously suppressed, but which came out more explicitly when he stifled his inhibitions with alcohol. He was prone to offering strange rambling stories that made no sense and seemed to go nowhere. He reveled in telling jokes that he'd crack up laughing to which had no evident punchline. His reputation shifted yet again. He had once been a respectable family man doing what he could to get by, but then he had become a drunk, ruining his poor family's life with his addiction. Now he emerged instead as a madman, a sort of village idiot for the Irish American community in Boston where he was well known as Kelley The Crackpot, often abbreviated to Kelley the Crack. It became a pastime for children to bait him into making bizarre statements before running off and laughing about it. It became the norm for every round bought in the bar to deliver a whiskey to his hands, a small price to pay for the entertainment to be found later in the evening when he started ranting and raving.

More and more pressure, not only for raising the children, but also for paying their way began falling on Bridget, and while she rose to the task with admirable determination, there simply weren't that many legal and moral ways for a woman to make a living for herself in the 1850s. Still, even as Peter slipped further and further into alcoholism and instability, they were getting by and making ends meet entirely thanks to her efforts.

Her willingness and steadfast determination to support and carry the household is why it was so crushingly devastating when she died. Tuberculosis was widespread in Boston, and down the whole east coast of America at the time, spreading most easily in damp warm places like the laundries where Bridget worked. Much of the workforce fell ill with the terrible disease. The pitiful sounds of coughing and hacking echoed through every part of the city, but nowhere so much as the cramped Irish neighbourhoods where conditions were at their worst and the disease had the easiest time spreading unchecked from one household to the next. Despite her sickness, Bridget worked on it. She toiled as the coughing wracked her body, as her muscles wasted away. She worked until she couldn't even stand by the vast cauldrons of boiling water and detergent that kept the clothes of the city clean without her daughter propping her up. Until the very end, she kept her sickness hidden from everyone so that she could continue working and keep her precious children from being tossed out into the street to die. Little Honora ended up as her nursemaid more often than not, as her older sisters attended school and did what they could to pretend that the horrors of home were not unfolding.

If Peter had been avoiding coming home before a horrible wasting illness took his wife, he was certainly in no hurry to get back there now. To sit, hungover, listening to the wet sounds of her hacking up blood while his mind struggled to decide whether it would be worse for it to keep on going, or for it to stop.

The choice was never in his hands. Bridget passed away in 1858. Just another number in the mounting death tolls of an epidemic that the wealthy and powerful didn't give a damn about. Better for the poor to die by the droves in their hovels than for them to go on being a drain on society. The Irish were the latest wave of demonised immigrants at the time, and many blamed them for bringing tuberculosis over from the old country and spreading it through the States. No tears were shed when yet another Catholic mother of too many children dropped dead of a sickness that seemed to be the destiny of every one of the Irish in Boston.

She was buried in a pauper's grave with no funeral to speak of, and if there was a wake, it was held exclusively by Peter and the bottle of whiskey he'd decided to treat himself to. Others mourned her, but they had no gathering place to do so in each other's company. As for the children, they were left alone in the dark of their apartment with no parents, no company and no hope for the future.

To his credit, Peter did try to do better for his children for a couple of years, at least. Unfortunately, "better" for Peter was still a fair distance short of the bare minimum needed. They were constantly on the verge of eviction, rarely had a meal a day and whatever guidance and support a parent was meant to impart to his children, Kelley the Crack was incapable of offering. At the very most, he took to work again with a little more seriousness, rebuilding his tailoring business at least to the point that he was entrusted with all the repairs from his dead wife's laundry. Perhaps it was out of sympathy for him and the memory of her, perhaps it was an attempt to keep his kids off the streets. Either way, it was sufficient to keep them alive for a while.

It was a tenuous peace, at best. Inside Peter, there was always the madness barely restrained. There was always the tremendous temptation to drink, to give in, to let it wash all his worries away even if it did make him back into the joke of the whole town. The drink had always let loose the worst of him, the chaos roiling behind his eyes, but now it was there, always simmering just beneath the surface, pressing against his restraint like a cracked dam.

The bedroom that had once belonged to Peter and his wife now became his refuge, his workspace and the place he'd seclude himself when the desire to drink came on too strong and he wanted to hide it from the children. When the door was shut, the message to all of them was clear, it was not to be opened, no matter what they heard from within. By this point, the older children had become essentially self-sufficient, dressing themselves and heading out to school, putting together whatever food there was in the house into meals or, if the pantry was bare, hounding their father on those occasions when he emerged from his room. Between them, they just barely survived. They heard their father sobbing in the night of course, but it wasn't a great surprise, since they had cried plenty of tears for their mother too. When he wailed and talked to himself, that wasn't so far outside of normal to raise any alarms, either. Children are nothing if not adaptable, and they had been exposed to more than enough of Peter's instability over the years for them to take it all in stride. All of them except for little Honora of course, who was the one trapped in their dingy apartment with him, day and night. Listening to him scream and rant to himself when he thought that there was nobody around to hear him. Doing her best not to take in any of the awful things that came tumbling out of his mouth once he was a few drinks into the day.

She was the one who had to endure his descent into darkness, who had to listen as he lost all tether to reality and wept over the awful world that he had made children come into. She was the one who broke the cardinal rule, the only real rule enforced in the house, not to open the door to daddy's room when it was shut.

He had gone quiet. Far too quiet. Even in his sleep Peter Kelley made enough racket snoring to wake the dead. But silence lay beyond the closed door of his bedroom and Honora was getting scared. What if he had died like mother had? What if he was dying now, and she could save him if she just went to check? He'd been crying and ranting, the way that he always had, but there had been the steady tug and pull of thread in cloth too, so he hadn't made it so far down the whiskey yet that he was insensible. She heard it still in the sudden silence that her father never gave her. That thrumming of thread, the sharp piercing of a needle slipping through, the faintest exhale as he pushed it to penetrate both layers he was seaming together. All that was missing was the customary cussing as he, in his clumsiness, occasionally poked himself with the needle.

She could hear him sew. Just as surely as if she were in the room with him, but he'd been drinking all morning, and he'd been slurring and gibbering all the way. Even at six years old Honora knew that her father could not have gone from that back to competence again so quickly. Something was wrong. Something was wrong, and she was too young to have the words to describe it. She was too young to know what to do. So, she followed the worst of her instincts, letting the mystery draw her closer she broke the one rule that they had, she opened the door.

Inside his room, Peter sat at his desk, with his back to the door. His hands were in motion, steady and fluid the way that they were when he was lost in his work. It must have been detailing, some minuscule stitch that he had to hold right up to his face to make out. Honora should have seen that and relaxed. She should have gone back out of the room without letting him know she'd broken the rule. She shouldn't have kept going once she knew everything was alright. But she was a child, and she needed comfort, even if the only one around to give it to her was entirely unqualified for the task. She stepped closer to her father, heard the twang of thread pulled taut and the soft exhalation as he began a new stitch. Something was still wrong. She couldn't put her finger on what, but there was still something frightening her. Still, something dragged her across to the worktable that had once been her mother's dresser. All the makeup was long gone and scraps of cloth were scattered everywhere. By the dim light of the oil lantern, she could see what appeared to be a rust-stained scrap of fabric by Peter's elbow.

There was a faint, high-pitched whine coming from her father, so high she couldn't have heard it if she weren't this close. This odd sound was somehow worse than the sobbing, worse than the ranting, at least those were still human things to do. This was an animal sound. A rabbit snared and helpless. A wolf gnawing off its own leg to escape. Pain beyond anything that words could express. Pain beyond what the human mind could comprehend. Honora didn't understand it, she didn't even know what that noise was, let alone what it meant. And through it all, still, Peter worked on, steady and rhythmic, every stitch in its place.

It was only when she finally came to be standing beside him, quaking in fear and uncertainty, that Honora finally saw what her father was sewing. There was no loose button being put back into place, or split seam being restitched. He had a needle and thread in his hand, but the only thing he was using it on was himself. He had already sewn one eye completely shut, and now he was midway through the other, working by touch and muscle memory alone. Needle piercing through skin, coming out trailing thread and red behind it.

If he saw Honora through what was left of that eye, nobody could guess, but when she screamed at the top of her lungs he heard her just fine. Whatever mania had possessed him to stitch shut his own eyes abandoned him just as quickly as it had come, and the screaming became two-sided. Both of them frantic and confused. It was as if someone else had done it to him. As if it was Honora's fault somehow. He flailed, he sobbed, he started pulling at the thread strung through his skin, the bleeding became a wash of red down his cheeks as stitches were torn. Little Honora, only six years old, had to be the one to grab his hands and stop him, sobbing and begging him to stop tearing the stitches out. It was up to her to find the scissors and press them into his hands, and she had to listen as he wailed between each snip, pulling thread across the surface of his eyeball to get it out.

He had to go see a doctor after that, leaving Honora all alone in the house until her sisters got home from school. They saw her, they saw the blood dried on her hands and the horrible stains in their father's sacrosanct room. They couldn't understand what had happened. Only that it was something terrible. She tried to explain, but the words came out muddled and confused. When their father finally arrived back home hours later with bandages across one eye and the other eye still a grotesque mess, they could see the damage but could make no sense of it.

Peter was still and silent on his return. Usually, it was a struggle to get a word in edgewise around him, but he remained uncharacteristically taciturn. It was only an hour or so later that the other men came. Official-looking men, with papers that they laid out in front of Peter which he signed without reading. Not that he could read half as well as any of his kids.

The children thought that this was the end, that their father was being consigned to some madhouse and would never return. If only that were so. It wasn't Peter being signed over into the care of the state. It was the children. He couldn't cope with the pressure. He couldn't manage a household. And while taking him in and trying to give him some sort of treatment might have helped Peter, the kids would have been left alone in the world without any caregiver. Something that even the shaky social construct of 1860s Boston would not tolerate. Delia and Honora would be going to the Boston Female Asylum. It was an institution where homeless or indigent children were warehoused until the state judged them capable of caring for themselves. A place where the state could profit off their misfortune, instead of having to pay out in charity. Their eldest sister Nellie escaped this terrible fate but was left to a potentially worse outcome. She would remain with their father as his caregiver.

Service and Virtue

Little information survives from the time that Honora was consigned to what was essentially a modern-day poorhouse. There are paper records from when she and her sister arrived, describing them as having been rescued from a miserable home life. Beyond that, little else is known. Their father Peter would never be heard from again by either of them. Over the years there were a bounty of various rumours circulated about him, none of which painted a happy fate for the man. Some said that he had killed himself while others purported that he had drunk himself into an early grave. It was even alleged that he'd beaten his poor daughter Nellie and left her for dead. Indeed, there was no shortage of grizzly speculation, none of which can be irrefutably confirmed or denied. As for the eldest sister, Nellie may have escaped a miserable stay in the Boston Female Asylum where her sisters Delia and Honora were placed, but she soon found her own unhappy circumstances as a homeless indigent, either having run away from the worst excesses of her father or as a result of him losing the apartment. Possibly even as a result of his early death.

Regardless, it would not be long before she too found herself in the care of the state. But unlike her little sisters whose stay in the Asylum would be only temporary, by the time that Nellie was confined, her sentence would be considerably more serious. She wasn't taken in to provide her with a home and a place in society, she was essentially arrested for being insane. What she could possibly have done to earn herself this diagnosis isn't clear, nor has any evidence survived beyond footnotes in the story of her sister as to what eventually became of her. It is possible that she inherited her father's mental illness and began showing symptoms as she reached the age of puberty, when schizophrenia typically manifests, but equally likely she may have just been indulging in anti-social behaviours that resulted in her being branded as mad. In strait-laced Boston society, almost anything that a woman could do independent of a man-made her the subject of derision and suspicion, and it is patently obvious that Nellie had no role models in her life to guide her away from such dangerous actions as might result in her being judged mentally improper in some way. Much like her father, this would be the last time that Nellie appeared in any sort of official records. In those days, being committed to a mental institute was less about treatment and more about containment. Keeping the undesirable elements of society hidden from sight where they cannot offend normal people. Few if any of the people who were taken into those facilities ever saw the light of day again, and the level of care that they received while incarcerated for life without any sort of legal trial can kindly be described as medieval. In those few places where the inhabitants weren't being actively tortured, they lived in vile conditions, suffered massive malnutrition and were generally hastened towards death by all means possible.

So two members of the family vanished into memory, and only Honora and Delia remained. In the dubious care of the Female Asylum, they would have been reliant on each other for essentially everything. With Honora being so young at a mere six years of age, she would have been an easy target for older bullies when her older sister wasn't around to protect her. Delia was only eight when they were taken into care, but she became the closest thing to a mother that Honora would ever remember in later life.

While Honora had no choice but to go with the programme, her older sister was a little more savvy about the way that the world worked. She recognised that the only reason she and her sister were imprisoned like they were was because they lacked the funds to buy themselves out of the situation. All of the kids in the Female Asylum were free to come and go as they pleased throughout the day, looking for whatever work they could find, or working the jobs that they had found. If they wandered off and never came back, it was a net savings for the state, so there would be no complaints until they were picked up by the police and returned, usually in an even more bedraggled state than they'd left in. Delia started to go out during the day and coming back with money. Not a lot of money, but more than a ten-year-old should have been able to earn for the hours that she'd been out and about. If the Asylum found out that any of its residents were making an income, then they'd be expected to contribute towards their own care, regardless of how young they were, so Delia kept it a secret from everyone but her sister. The manner in which this child was earning her money would not come to light for almost a year, by which time she had managed to accumulate a not insignificant amount of cash. Not enough to get her and her sister a place outside of the Asylum, but well on the way to a nest egg large enough that they might be able to get their lives back on track. Of course, that was when she finally ran afoul of the police.

It would have been more palatable to her keepers at the Asylum if she had been stealing. Picking pockets was almost accepted as the norm among the residents, particularly the young ones who could typically avoid suspicion by virtue of their age, but Delia had gotten herself involved in something much worse than that. She was committing crimes which a child of her age should not have even been aware of, let alone become a participant in. At eleven years old, Delia was a known prostitute.

This presented a problem for the Asylum. While they were willing to take in urchins, beggars and other miscellaneous criminals, a prostitute was another matter. It could besmirch the good name of their institution and bring shame on them all for living there and working alongside young ladies of questionable virtue. There had, of course, been many young women down on their luck and willing to trade in flesh and risk their immortal souls for a chance to escape the asylum, and for them, the procedure had always been clear. They were turned over to the police as soon as evidence of their wrongdoing came to light, and they were banished forthwith from the Asylum. But eleven-year-old Delia presented a conundrum. This was a child, who clearly could not have made these horrendous decisions alone. Clearly, they could not realistically expect her to serve any time in an adult prison nor could she live alone on the streets, either would be tantamount to a death sentence. So, where normally there would have been condemnation and banishment, Delia experienced a very quiet meeting with members of the board where an agreement was reached. She would leave the asylum, they would allow her to keep her ill-gotten gains and they would all act as if they did not know one another or anything about what had occurred. It was the best offer that Delia was liable to get, but it came with a terrible price. She had enough money to support herself, at least in the short term, but there wasn't enough cash that she could buy her sister out of the Asylum too. If she left, it would be on the condition of having no further contact with Honora. In effect, she was abandoning Honora to whatever nightmares awaited her. It would have been an awful choice for anyone to make, but for a child, it was a particularly cruel decision to have foisted on her. Delia gave in. She folded. There was nothing else that she could do, the other side held all the cards and all that she had was her money, money which could all too easily have been confiscated from her. Even after the awful things that she'd done to get it.

There was no opportunity for tearful goodbyes. She did not get to see her little sister one last time to explain to the seven-year-old what was happening. Perhaps it would have been even more brutal if she had. Instead, Delia simply vanished from Honora's life, leaving the little girl stranded and abandoned by everyone she had ever known and loved; leaving her as the last of the Kelley clan and the only member whose story we are still able to follow.

Alone in the Asylum, Honora did poorly. She was too small to muscle in when there was food, so she grew smaller still. She was too soft to force others to obey her, so she became a background player in her own life, following the demands of the bigger tougher girls and fading ever more. She didn't know where her family had gone, or what had happened to cause their lives to fall apart so completely. Given her tender young age, it seems unlikely that she could have grasped the answers even if they had been given to her. From one hell, it seemed she had fallen into another, even deeper and without any hope of escape.

At least, that is how it seemed during that one dark year when she was alone, lost and confused. The staff at the Asylum may not have been bleeding hearts by any stretch of the imagination, but they could see the situation that the little girl was in, and they wanted her out of it. Whether that was because of kindness, or because of the potential profit that there was to be made from a biddable and compliant urchin didn't much matter in the end. Two years after arriving in the care of the state, Honora was ejected from it with just as little care or kindness. She was eight years old when the carriage came to the orphanage door to collect her, and after spending her entire life in one long ongoing downward spiral, it should come as no surprise that she treated this new twist in her tale with some trepidation. The driver was not unkind, but neither was he particularly welcoming, or intent on explaining himself to some little tot with more muck on her than his horses. It would only be when he delivered her to the Toppan family home that her future began to become a little clearer.

There was snow drifting down as the carriage pulled up outside the Toppan house and Honora had been drifting in and out of sleep the whole way. It was a thirty-mile trip from Boston out to the outlying town of Lowell. It was the furthest that the little girl had ever travelled in her life but being so small and confused she remembered little of the trip, caught in a kind of twilight state with the early sunset and her own exhaustion. When the doors to the grand house opened, Honora knew without a doubt that there had been some mistake. She could not have been the girl that this family was looking for. Their home was like a fairy tale, with paintings on the walls, polished wooden floors, carpets and wallpaper and so many more luxuries that it would never have even occurred to Honora that she might one day encounter them. It was a beautiful home, pristinely kept and warm. Honora couldn't remember ever being warm before. In the dead of summer, their apartment had been roasting hot, but the rest of the time memory only ever brought her memories of shivering against the bitter cold and huddling close to her long-gone sisters in the single bed they shared. In the Asylum, she had not even had that. Stepping inside the hallway only because the driver had pushed her forward, she almost tripped over her own feet. She felt like she was sullying this beautiful place just by being here. As if the stains of her past life might soak out into the rugs. But from the hand of one servant, she was passed into the hands of another.

The woman in the grand house was kind and gentle, leading the little girl through to the servants' quarters, drawing her a bath and laying out fresh clothes for her to wear, since her old ones would tragically be heading for the incinerator. Still, Honora couldn't grasp what was going on and she was too afraid to ask. Because she went along with everything so easily, everyone was assuming that she knew ahead of time what was going to come to pass. The truth of the matter, however, was that she had no idea what to expect but experience had long ago taught her that going with the flow and asking no questions was the best way to avoid trouble, and she so desperately wanted to avoid trouble. There had obviously been some mistake in bringing her here, and she had no doubt that she'd be punished for her indiscretions upon her return to the asylum, but for now, she could not resist the temptations laid out before her. A bath, clean clothes, hot food, a bed, an actual bed with a mattress and pillow, all for her. She couldn't believe the good fortune that she'd fallen into, and she was intent on keeping her mouth shut for as long as she possibly could to ensure that she got as much time as possible to enjoy this luxury before the mistake was discovered and she was banished back to the pit.

Yet despite all of the obvious comfort and her affirmations to herself that she must make the most of things, Honora struggled to settle into sleep that night. There was nobody trying to kick her or steal her blanket, and there was nobody coughing that racking bloody cough that had taken her mother, in fact, there was an almost blissful stillness and silence to the whole building, but it was strange. Honora had lived in a slum for most of her life, and a poorhouse for the rest, even the most basic levels of comfort were alien to her. In the end, she slipped down off the bed and slept on the more familiar hard floorboards. She would get over this sense of being a fish out of water eventually, but it wouldn't be on her first night in the house. Nor would it be on the first day of the new life that she had just been dropped into without even being asked.

It was only when morning came and she was settled for breakfast with the other servants of the house that the full picture of what had brought Honora here became clear, and even then only because the maid was explaining it to the driver who'd brought her the night before.

Honora was going to be an indentured servant to the owners of the house. Essentially a slave. She would not receive any payment for her labour, with some monies being sent instead to the institute that had provided her and contracted her out. To begin with, she would serve only as another maid around the house, though there was an expectation that she might grow into a more prominent role, perhaps as the personal servant to the young mistress, since the pair were so closely matched in age. For now, she'd be turning down beds, restocking fireplaces, sweeping, dusting, mopping and anything else that was asked of her, the very moment that it was asked of her. The other servants need not have worried, Honora was nothing if not compliant and obedient. She would do precisely as she was told from the very moment that she was told to do it.

Her first day was spent shadowing the regular maid, learning all of her duties with a brief break for lunch. The owners of the house, the Toppan family, were out doing business in Boston at the moment, so there was time enough for Honora to learn without her causing any disruption to the natural order of things in the house. By the time that the family returned, Honora was well settled into her role, surprising all the other servants with how quickly she had mastered all of her tasks and could be set to the next. While for them, this was work, for the little girl, it was an escape from the nightmares of her past, an opportunity to prove that she was worth more than the nothing that she'd always been treated like. While she lacked the physical strength to take on some of the more onerous tasks of the house, she learned far faster than anyone could have expected and was picking up more and more every day.

Of course, the real test of her staying power would have nothing to do with her ability to act as a servant. Any number of children in the asylum could have done that, even if they would have done it with markedly less dogged determination and grace. The real test to decide whether Honora was going to fit in with the family was Elizabeth.

The master and mistress of the house had a young daughter, almost exactly the same age as their new servant, and if she decided that she did not like this new girl, then her tenure in the Toppan house would surely be short-lived.

Elizabeth met Honora on her first night back from Boston. She was quite startled by the presence of another little girl in her room, lighting the fire to keep her warm through the November night. For her part, Honora looked like nothing more than a little doll. A tiny maid's uniform stitched perfectly to size for her by someone far more skilled and better paid than her father ever had been. Honora averted her gaze from the mistress of the house, even though the mistress was only eight, but she was invited over all the same.

In a strange way, the two girls were alike in ignorance. Elizabeth had been sheltered from all the terrible things that could happen to a girl her age by her comfortable circumstances, while Honora had remained blissfully ignorant of everything beyond the surface-level horrors that she'd experienced, with all that was worse sinking deep below the surface of her awareness. That first meeting was inevitably awkward, with neither girl having much of a clue how to talk to the other, but they soon fell into a comfortable rhythm with Honora going about her tasks and delighting in hearing about her new friend's day. The books that she'd read, the studies she'd undertaken and the places that she'd been. Honora had not grown up enough yet for her heartbreaking circumstances to make her bitter. She treated every joy that Elizabeth received as a delight to be enjoyed herself, secondhand. Even as the pair of them began to grow, it would be together rather than apart. With each passing month, Elizabeth seemed to love her little maid all the more, and there was no question that someday Honora would have pride of place in the household as her lady's first servant. Such obvious adoration from those who lived upstairs could have driven a wedge between Honora and the other servants, but once again, her innocence protected her from suspicions of trying to curry favour, and they came to care for her too, in their own way. Indentured or not, she was soon taking on the work of an adult maid, tackling so many duties around the house that the pressure eased off the rest of the staff. They told her not to push so hard, that there was no benefit in it, but Honora still set herself to every task with determination to be the best and to do the most that she could. Gradually her education began, a combination of offhand lessons passed along by Elizabeth, and a more deliberate effort by those who lived downstairs to get her up to speed, capable of reading, writing and mathematics at the very least. The Toppans had a generous policy about lending from their library to servants, so it took barely any time before Honora was reading at a level that would put many children in the modern age to shame.

Elizabeth came to occupy more and more of her time, and her heart, also. Her other duties would always come second to whatever the little girl wanted of her. Gradually, as it became apparent she wouldn't be punished for doing so, Honora acquiesced to join in with her lessons when a tutor arrived, to coming first thing in the day to help her mistress get dressed, and to prepare her hair, and all manner of other little kindnesses that servants who dote on their masters indulge in. The chef's menu might change to include a sweet treat that Elizabeth had mentioned was her favourite. The dressmaker might stitch her clothes in a fashion that appealed less to her parents' conservative tastes and more to those of their daughter. They were doting parents, as loving as Honora was proving to be towards their daughter, so they saw no harm in any of these changes and came to appreciate all that their little girlmaid was trying to do to make their daughter's life better.

Honora served as Elizabeth's bridge to the lower levels of society where everything actually got done, while Elizabeth served as Honora's bridge to high society, education and the possibilities of a brighter future.

All of this came to an abrupt halt when Elizabeth sickened. A fever had her laid up in bed and she was confined to her rooms by her doctors lest any sickness spread. At almost the very same moment, Honora seemed to vanish from her daily duties, as she occasionally did when sent on an errand by her mistress. It would only be later that it became apparent she had gone into quarantine with the other girl, risking her own health so that she could nurse Elizabeth through the worst of her illness. If they had been close before, now they became sisters in everything but blood.

While she was never formally adopted by the Toppans, they were more than happy for Honora to take on their family name as her own. They knew a little of her history before she had come to them, and they gathered early on that there was no love lost between her and her father who had, in Honora's mind, abandoned all of his children. Anything that the Toppans could do to help her distance herself from that man sounded like a splendid idea. At Elizabeth's suggestion, Honora also started going by a different forename as well, cutting herself off from her Irish Catholic heritage, and presenting her with all the opportunities that would come from an Anglicised Protestant name like Jane Toppan.

Jane was essentially a new person; a girl granted a fresh start who was rapidly approaching the end of the period of her indentured service. A girl who had prospects and a future. A young man from town began courting her, gifting her a ring in the shape of a bird with the promise that the two of them would be wed. It would be months after he left town that news finally reached Jane that he'd married his landlady's daughter out west.

This tipped Jane into a depression, and she destroyed the bird ring, melting it in the kitchen fireplace. This marked the end of her romantic life.

Two suicide attempts would follow in the coming months. Both by the reckless ingestion of drugs in such doses that a smaller girl would most certainly have been killed, but Jane was built larger than the average woman and made of sterner stuff. She bounced back from each of her attempts on her own life with renewed vigour. Back on her feet and back to work so swiftly that her brief bouts of "illness" could be set aside as nothing more than a common cold.

With the long history of mental illness in her family, this might seem like the breaking point at which Jane's previously pleasant personality flipped and she became some sort of maniacal murderer, but the only real change in her behaviour and demeanour was a newfound belief in prophetic dreams. She would sit with Elizabeth for hours, pouring over the journals that the two of them kept of their dreams and trying to divine the future from them. Her attempts at foretelling the future did not prove to be particularly successful, even if they did entertain her adoptive sister for quite some time. Jane was desperate to find something, anything, in life that was just hers. She craved something that made her feel special, like someone more than just some lowborn nobody. The giggles from Elizabeth when her predictions came to nothing felt like knives buried in her back. At that point, Jane abandoned her pursuit of spiritualism and returned to her mundane duties as a maid.

In an attempt to brighten her mood back up, when Jane reached her 18th birthday, Mrs Ann Toppan made a princely gift of fifty dollars to the girl, explaining it was a nest egg that she could use to start herself out in the world. Establishing herself as whatever she wanted to be and doing whatever she wanted to do.

Despite her generous endowment, Jane remained with the Toppan family, and more specifically with Elizabeth, as a paid servant for almost a decade following her eighteenth birthday when she could have walked free. She seemed to enjoy the work for the most part, though she definitely began to slack on her household duties a little as the years went by. She was in a curious position, between the upstairs and downstairs, and she no longer had her childish innocence to protect her from the discomforts that caused.

Jane had attended school alongside Elizabeth after private tutors proved ineffective. She was often treated like a foster sister, and she received as good an education as any young woman at that time was likely to receive in Massachusetts. Regardless of the opportunities such an education could provide, there didn't seem to be any ambition in her to do more than live out her days by Elizabeth's side. Unfortunately, there was a slowly developing wedge growing between them, and despite her most determined efforts, Jane didn't seem to be capable of patching that gap.

The trouble was that Jane was a liar. She had always been a liar for so long as Elizabeth knew her, telling tall tales from her own past to amuse her adoptive sister. As the girls grew older, however, the lies stopped being entertaining and simply became baffling. Elizabeth knew that Jane's father didn't live in China and that her family had not died at sea, so why on earth would the woman tell her such blatant lies. As clever as Jane was, she never seemed to be quite smart enough to keep her mouth shut. She alienated the other servants with the same sort of storytelling as was poisoning her relationship with Elizabeth and increasingly felt like she was at a dead end. It was as though the lies were an attempt to rewrite her past so that she knew which route to follow forward. When Jane reached the age of twenty-five, Mrs Toppan once again attempted to push her gently but firmly out the door, after all, she already had one daughter to contend with and didn't need a second one sprouting up from the servants' quarters like a fungus.

Elizabeth was in the midst of marriage proposals and suitors by this point, with Jane scowling on, inventing tales of how those suitors were unsuited to her, about their lecherous stares and their rude comments behind Elizabeth's back. It only took being tricked by Jane about these matters a couple of times before Elizabeth's relationship with Jane soured entirely. Jane had been trying to keep her 'sister' to herself and instead had driven her even further away.

Oramel Brigham was a deacon at the church that the Toppans attended and shortly before the death of Elizabeth's mother, he made his proposal and it was accepted. He was to move into the Toppan house with Elizabeth and make it their marital home. Something that Jane could not abide the thought of. There was this girl who she had cared for since she was little more than a baby, a girl that she'd loved like her own blood, and she was expected to just stand aside and let this vile ingrate violate her? She wasn't going to stand for it. She wasn't going to stay under the same roof as these horrors unfolded. She was done.

Truly unhappy with her lot in life for the first time since the Toppans rescued her from the nightmare of the Asylum, Jane was forced to take the first proactive step in her life to change things. Thanking the Toppan family for their hospitality, she departed their home when she was almost thirty years old. She left with a suitcase full of clothes and a wad of cash that would have made anyone in the working class envious, but she had no idea of what she was going to do with herself for the rest of her life.

Jolly Jane

Careers were not widely available to women in 1885, a time when women were rarely seen as much more than accessories for their husbands or caregivers, but Jane's excellent education with the Toppans and her experience as a maid actually proved to be a great boon. Before she had been out of the family home for more than a short while, she found her feet, beginning training as a nurse at Cambridge Hospital.

She was well-liked in the hospital, where her positive attitude and general cheer helped to counterbalance the serious nature of their work. Her experience from her earlier career meant that she had no issue with getting her hands dirty where other higher-born nurses might have flinched away, and she had already built up the physical strength that was required to perform her duties before she had even begun having to haul patients around.

While the morbidity of some of the tasks required of them drove many of her fellow students into depression, Jane's own hard life seemed to have made her markedly more resilient and capable of getting through the worst days without her smile ever faltering. If anything, as things got darker, she seemed to glow all the brighter. As if she relished the challenges of the work and the challenge of keeping everyone around her happy while she set herself to it. Before long, she had received the nickname "Jolly Jane" that would follow her throughout the rest of her medical career.

While some of the nurses were quite content to serve as glorified housemaids for the hospital, changing beds and providing sponge baths, Jane and a cohort of other more ambitious young women took their studies of medicine considerably more seriously. While she would never receive the full education that would have been required to make her a doctor due to the sexism of the day blocking her from entry to higher education, she pursued her interest in the subject on her own time, reading many of the texts that would have informed a doctor's medical school education. She might not have been able to sit in on lectures, but all of the information that was being imparted in those lectures was available in the teaching hospital's library, and she absorbed it at a rate that would have made many a doctor envious. In terms of practical lessons on how procedures were carried out, Jane had a front-row seat to the majority of them, and it would not be long before the doctors were entrusting her with certain tasks beyond the simple administering of medicine. As for the practical aspects of anatomical lessons that she was missing out on, there was no shortage of dead bodies being autopsied in the morgue to examine them for their cause of death, and she was able to spend what free time she had throughout the day observing there too. Gradually her education reached the point that she had as good a working understanding of medicine as many of the doctors who worked in the hospital, and as such, had made herself an incredible asset to the institution.

She was trusted with almost every task shy of surgery by this point, and even some minor surgeries that would be conducted on the ward were often left in her capable hands. She was older than many of the other nurses, even those who had been working at the hospital for years, and soon the sense that they had of seniority over her began to turn upside down. If there was a question or a crisis, it was Jolly Jane that was turned to as the first port of call, with the doctors only being summoned when she couldn't come up with a solution.

Legally, she could not prescribe medicine to any of their patients, but for the most part, she would administer what was necessary for the patient's wellbeing and then have a doctor sign off on it after the fact to save friction. Despite only spending a few years at the hospital, allegedly as a trainee, she was looked to by everyone around her with respect and trust.

Much like when she had first been cast in the role of maid by her 'adoption,' she had done all that she could to prove herself worthy of her new position and to ingratiate herself with those around her. There was no nurse that hadn't felt the comforting hand of Jolly Jane on their shoulder during a difficult shift, leading them off to get a cup of tea and settle their nerves. There was no doctor who didn't let out a little sigh of relief that she was there when she could offer a medical history of the patient with a degree more insight than any chart might have managed. The patients came to love her too, or at least to rely on her heavily. She was the nurse with the strong arms who could get them sat up, who could wipe away their messes without a look of disgust. The nurse who would press a kiss to their feverish foreheads and promise that everything would be okay and then slip them a little painkiller to make it feel like the lie might be true.

Her birth family might have abandoned her, her foster family might have cast her out as surplus to requirements, but here there would always be people who needed her. People who not only wanted her company for the joy that she brought but who literally relied upon her to keep them alive. Nobody here could reject her. Nobody here could tell her that she wasn't loved enough. There was no doom hanging overhead just waiting to fall the moment that she was judged to be less than perfect. But she pursued perfection all the same because it made them love her even more. Small wonder that she spent all of her time with a smile plastered on her face when she had finally found an adoptive family that couldn't get away from her. The deepest cut on her psyche, recently reopened by Elizabeth's rejection of her in favour of seeking a husband, could finally begin to heal. And what that would leave behind would be a twisted mass of scar tissue.

Everyone had power over Jane, and Jane had no power over anyone.

She was a woman, marginalised and weak, incapable of being considered an equal to any man in the world despite having the strength and intellect to match any one of them. She was a commoner in a subsection of a world dominated by the wealthy upper class that was even more dominated by the wealthy upper class, spending all of her time seeing just how thoroughly they detested people like her. She felt she had to constantly hide her heritage and humble beginnings to avoid being on the receiving end of their contempt. The rich and the powerful received the best treatment while the rest were left to rot in the lower wards. Places where Jolly Jane rarely had to venture nowadays, since by her excellence she'd been claimed for the better class of clientele.

All of her life, she had walked the knife's edge between her past, and the threat of being damned back to it if she failed to be acceptable enough, and her present among the wealthy and beautiful. Leaning too far in either direction would have led to her immediate destruction. When she tried to act too much like a sister to the rich girl whose family had taken her in as a servant, she was banished. Conversely, had spent her time lounging among the servants downstairs in the evenings, she would have lost her position and influence, and been doomed to an eternity living downstairs among the poor and the pitiable.

It was a hell of her own making. One she could have escaped at any time if she were willing to sink back down into poverty and degradation, to become a whore or a madwoman or sit in a dark room slurping whiskey and sewing piece-work until she took the needles to her own face. If she had been willing to just become the nothing that she was meant to be, then there would have been no trouble at all. It was only in striving for better that she found suffering. It was only because she wanted more than to be nobody that she had to suffer the terrible indignity of those around her commenting on the nobodies that she was choosing not to be.

Powerless all her life, she now found herself in the opposite position. The patients in the hospital were entirely in her power. If she chose to withhold their medication, they would die. If she chose to inject them with more than they were meant to receive, or even to fiddle with their charts a little so that someone else would, she could snatch life away from any one of them. From being an Irish drunkard's daughter worthy of nothing more than pity and disgust, she had come to hold the power of God in her hands, deciding between life and death for each and every one of her patients.

She enjoyed dipping the patients in her care in and out of consciousness more or less hourly, just to see what different combinations of medications could do. She would choose favourites from among the patients on her wards and lavish extra attention on them, in part to keep up the façade of 'Jolly Jane' the kindly nurse, but more to keep close watch over them as she performed her experiments with their treatment. Mostly these were patients without close families, elderly people whose death would create no great stir, but amongst them, she would cotton on to certain other victims for no real reason at all that could be deciphered. Maybe she simply liked the look of them. Maybe they made some comment that she took kindly, or unkindly to. Enough information about these early victims simply isn't available, because it is impossible to say precisely when she first killed, or even if it was a deliberate choice on her part. Perhaps she was simply playing around with dosages a little and the unfortunate result was a patient expiring.

She would spend her free time in the hospital with her guinea pigs, watching over them, altering their charts so that they'd continue to receive the medication regimen that she prescribed them and even going so far as to climb into bed with some of them so that she could feel up close the effects that her experiments were having on them. She could feel their rattling breaths as they struggled against the morphine. She could feel their temperatures rising as she dosed them with atropine. Every condition under the sun was treated in Cambridge Hospital, and she got front-row seats to not only every one of them, but to every variation of them that she could manipulate.

Death was a constant in the hospital, and for the duration of her residency there, as Jane studied for her full nursing qualification, she was surrounded by it. The rich and the powerful were helpless in the face of death, the only ones with the courage to face it head-on were the doctors and she found them to be almost laughably fallible. So many of them were self-assured in every decision that they made despite the research that informed their decisions being years out of date. The smart ones, the truly smart ones, who could recognise their own limitations, would refer to Jane to help confirm treatments and diagnoses as she continued her learning long past the point of reason and all the way over the edge into obsession. They would come to her, and ask her advice, and she'd give it, and those doctors would find few surprises with their patients. But the others, who talked over her and ignored her, their patients seemed to have worse luck. It wasn't that Jane was deliberately killing them. She didn't need to. The doctors were doing that for her.

Yet amongst the constant flux of the living and the dead, some portion of those who passed away did so under Jane's direct care. She held their hand as the life slipped away from them. She worked frantically when she could to bring them back from the brink. She held her face inches from theirs as they drew their final breath. These were people who had never known a moment of hardship in their life, who had all the wealth and comfort that life could bring, but in the end, they came under her stewardship and when offered the choice between letting them live or die, she chose what pleased her the most.

Sex had more or less entirely passed Jane by in her life. Her fiancé from her younger days had abandoned her before anything could come to fruition in that department and now she was once again walking the knife edge of propriety. There was no shortage of young attractive nurses walking away from their work with a husband that they'd nursed back to health, many pairing off with the doctors who were meant to be their teachers in the hospital. Bastard offspring of such unions were a constant, but in these higher echelons of society, there were mechanisms in place to protect the dubious honour of the men who impregnated them. The nurses would simply vanish. Allegedly travelling or visiting some elderly relative who had sickened. There would be no comment upon their absence. She was not going to succumb to the doctors' advances, even if those advances were mostly from very viable bachelors who in no small part were drawn to her out of ambition to secure her as their own personal research assistant. From one prison to the next, she would not be beholden to anyone ever again.

Due to this lack of an outlet for her more base instincts, it should come as little surprise that pleasure found its way to her in other ways. When she first started to kill patients, it was most likely accidental as she toyed with their medication, then when it became more deliberate, the enjoyment that she gained from the slaughter was more likely to be a delight at the exercise of her personal power over them. The exact moment that enjoyment of power over life and death began to intermingle with sexual enjoyment is as hard to pinpoint as anything else in this quiet and mostly undocumented part of her life. But intermingle the feelings did. The sight of a patient in their death throes began to arouse her. The moment of their death became the moment that she experienced what the French call the "little death" of orgasm.

Now the long and arduous torments that she put her patients through, taking them to the very edge of death before bringing them back was no longer an experiment in seeing how close to oblivion she could take someone before dragging them back. Now it was foreplay, and the longer that she toyed with a victim, the better it felt.

Before she had been in a dalliance with death, a little flirtation with it here and there, but with this latest development, the excitement of killing became her entire purpose for being. To feel content and satisfied in her life, probably for the first time, she had to kill. She had to feel. In a world that denied her and all women any sexual autonomy, she had found a way to bypass all of the dangers that might have led to her dismissal from her position.

In 1887, barely more than a year into her residency, it seemed that she had made the connection between the sexual and caregiving aspects of herself. A patient named Amelia Phinney emerged from an operation and anaesthesia to find Jane in bed with her, kissing her all over her face, her neck, her lips. In a hazy state of bare awareness, Amelia made some sound of complaint, and that seemed enough to startle Jane out of her frenzy. She administered a bitter-tasting medicine to Amelia, and the woman faded back out of awareness.

In all the years that followed, Amelia Phinney told nobody about the strange dream that she had when coming out of surgery, for fear that the mere thought of it might paint her as a pervert, fantasising about a nurse climbing into bed with her and doing such things. It would only be much later when the truth came out that she would finally realise that she, like so many others, had been molested by Jane while they were sleeping.

And then, as abruptly as Jane had found her perfect state of being, it was over. Her training at the hospital over the latter months of her residency had mostly just been her teaching others, having long since surpassed any of the material lessons that were required for her job, and there was a fresh wave of new nursing students coming in. As much as many of the doctors campaigned to keep Jane on the staff permanently, there simply wasn't a position available for her at the time, so they did the best that they could by her, writing her an absolutely glowing recommendation to the most prestigious hospital in the area, Massachusetts General.

She began working there in 1889, carrying over all the goodwill from her last position and being immediately accepted and appreciated by the staff of the new hospital. Things were at a different speed in Mass General, while there had been a degree of chaos at work in her previous hospital due to all the students, life was considerably more restrictive at her new job. Little mistakes or miscalculations, wastage of medication, these were all relatively commonplace in a teaching hospital, but now it became necessary for Jane to abide strictly to the letter of the rules instead of just their spirit. If less medicine was administered to a patient than had been prescribed, then a simple check on stocks would show it. If more medicine was administered, then its absence would draw attention. She had to adapt, and it took her longer than she had anticipated to do so. Instead of coming and going as she pleased and doing as she pleased during those comings and goings, she was now on a tight rotation of wards and shifts that she had to abide by if she meant to keep her position.

While it might have seemed that these restrictions should have interfered with her hobby, she was still more than capable of doctoring charts to result in the medicine being administered in compliance with her demands rather than those of the patient's needs. As to the careful watch kept on medical supplies, it was a simple enough matter for her to begin balancing the books. She learned to waste excess medicine when she wanted to reduce a dosage and to save up the excesses she accrued by reducing some patient's medication and giving it to those she chose. It was a layer of complexity that she wasn't accustomed to managing, but one that she dealt with quite readily. Throughout her tenure at Cambridge Hospital, she had become accustomed to being the smartest person in the room, and despite the quality of staff at her new hospital, she was still under the impression that she was entirely untouchable.

This was not the case.

As patients under her care began to die, typically when they were completely alone with her, a pattern began to emerge. The other nurses may not have all had her degree of education, but they were not stupid or inexperienced the way that many of the student nurses had been. When Jolly Jane was acting strangely, they took note of it.

None of this is to say that anyone suspected her of what she was actually doing. If anyone noticed a pattern of death in the patients that Jane took a special interest in, then they normally flipped the causation in their mind. This kindly nurse who came to them with only the highest of praise was obviously spotting the patients who were in the greatest need of comfort because they were on their way out the door and she was simply trying to offer them that comfort. Her extra care and attention couldn't possibly have been the cause of their early demise. Some people take refuge in audacity, joking about things so extreme that nobody could ever take them seriously. Jane took refuge in the fact that nobody had even considered the possibility that a nurse might be a murderer.

And why would they? Nurses were angels of mercy. The bravest members of the fairer sex, willing to endure the unseemly indelicacies that were required to help save lives. Well perhaps not save lives, but nurse those who'd already been saved by reliable and intelligent men back to fighting fitness. To be a murderer would have required a degree of competence that society did not afford to women.

But it was that very doubt of her competence that was eventually Jane's undoing. For two years she worked diligently at Massachusetts General, performing her duties with care and impressing everyone with her knowledge of medicine, in particular pharmaceuticals. But in a world where women were considered to be scarcely more intelligent than beasts of burden, it should come as little surprise that her own competence was eventually questioned. Enough of her patients had died under her care that some suspicion had begun to mount. Enough of her peers had grown jealous of her reputation among the higher staff of the hospital that whispers began to spread. Eventually, a whisper in the right ear led to an autopsy being performed on one of her victims and a lethal dose of morphine was found in their system.

There was no allegation of impropriety on her part, no hint that she might have deliberately overdosed a patient to kill them, only the condemnation of her competence. She was too flippant in her jolliness. Too carefree when it came to caring for those on the brink of death. Her soft heart had obviously led her to this. Slipping the patient extra medication to ease their pain because she loved them all so much. She was dressed down for her mishandling of dangerous medications and dismissed.

In any sane world, this would, of course, have been the end of the matter. Her reputation as a nurse would have been ruined and her career ended. Unfortunately, she did not live in a sane world, but one governed by propriety. It would not do for any news of a nurse killing patients to escape the hospital grounds. It could damage the public's trust in medicine, leading to far more deaths when they would not subject themselves to treatment. It could lead to uproar and lawsuits from the families of those that had died under Jane's care resulting in the bankruptcy of the hospital and the subsequent loss of their ability to care for others being stripped away from them, one dollar at a time. It was an embarrassment to an institution that prided itself on its reputation, so Jane was released from her service without any reason as to why being provided.

Once more the exact number of people that fell victim to her is impossible to determine, not only because of all the legitimate routine deaths that befell the patients in the hospital but also because the full breadth of her mishandling of medication was never discovered. She did not merely experiment with doping patients up on opiates, there was a whole medicine cabinet of toys for her to play with, and she had dipped into every bottle in Massachusetts General to keep herself entertained. The damage that she did to the patients she toyed with could have killed many of them instantly while giving other people conditions that would plague them for the remainder of their lives, however long that might be. A veritable cocktail of different medications had been mis-administered by Jolly Jane as she played with the patients' lives. Interestingly, many of the patients that she had personally treated suffered no ill effects, even the ones that she had drugged the most prodigiously. Just because her gentle attentions could lead to death or sickness didn't mean that they often did. Quite the opposite in fact. For every one person that died so that she could feel an orgasmic rush, there were hundreds who survived thanks to her diligent efforts and intelligence. There was no fun in playing with life-and-death stakes if every game ended in death. If she wanted wholesale slaughter, it would have been all too easy to achieve. She could have bounced joyously through the wards administering lethal doses of morphine to every single patient before anyone thought to stop her. The joy was in the game. The interplay of possibilities. Keeping her victims on the edge of death was the font of her enjoyment, and saving the vast majority of them just reinforced, at least in Jane's own mind, just how powerful she truly was.

The new hospital, with its more focused staff, was a less-than-ideal environment to continue with her experiments and self-exploration, so following her dismissal, the next stop for her seemed fairly obvious. She went straight back to Cambridge Hospital in 1890 and, to the great delight of everyone who had worked with her before, took one of the more senior nursing roles that didn't get doled out to mere students. Like a returning hero, she was ushered back into the wards she had walked as a new resident, armed with all of the experience and confidence that she had garnered in her travels. It did not take long before she was back into her usual routine. Beloved by some of the staff and prickling the nerves of those who didn't care for her arrogant attitude. Of course, those who considered her to be arrogant were among the most genuinely arrogant doctors on the staff. Such men would have been put out by any woman with her degree of competence, but unlike other nurses who thought that they knew better than the doctors – and had the knowledge to back it up – Jane came to them with an inherent flaw that they could use against her, even if they weren't yet aware of it. That flaw, of course, being that she was a mass murderer.

For several months she sank back into the usual routine and did her best not to make waves, remembering how everything was done and how much one could get away with before alarms sounded. She tested out the safety net designed to protect patients from overenthusiastic students in the teaching hospital and discovered that they were actually quite a bit more robust than she had initially realised. Her chart modifications from before had avoided notice not because she had been so devilishly clever, but primarily because the symptoms that she had induced were expected of the patients based on their particular maladies. Now that she was no longer a student, and as such was hands-on with practically every aspect of the ward, she had to be far more careful in picking her victims.

Another red flag that was soon raised about her return was the length of time she would spend assisting in the mortuary, even though it was hardly one of the duties expected of her. It seemed to an outside observer to be some sort of morbid obsession. She was either morbidly fixated upon the dead in general, or falling into the obsessive spiral that marked the death knell of so many medical careers, when she went over her mistakes again and again, sitting in on the autopsies of those who had died in her care out of guilt or fixation on correcting herself in the future. In fact, neither was entirely true. She spent her time in the morgue with her victims, because seeing them dead and carved up added to her enjoyment. Each time she hovered over the slab, holding up a lamp for the coroner, or prying back a flap of skin so that another organ could be examined, she was getting to relive her murder. Toying with the corpses of their victims is a relatively common behaviour for serial killers, and Jane was no different. Of course, with Jane being the bastion of practicality that she was, her presence, lingering over the bodies of her victims long past the point that they had departed this mortal coil, also served another purpose. If there was anything in the autopsy that might have provoked suspicion of her, she was there, ready to hide it, to interfere with tests, to edit the reports, to adjust the weights, to cover her tracks. It was sufficient to make even those who trusted her implicitly a little concerned, and that small smudge of doubt was the wedge that those who didn't like her could use to pry apart the overwhelming trust in the nurse.

As a student, some margin for error was allowed, but as a fully-fledged nurse, the doctors who looked down on her could pick at every decision she made and every drop of medicine she administered. Despite being under that obscene degree of scrutiny, Jane never once let her mask of joviality slip, never once let anyone see the pressure that she was being put under, she toddled along about her day as happy as could be, doing everything that she was supposed to do and more, as if there was a way for her to prove to those that hated her that she was worthy of their respect, simply by continuing to be the best possible version of herself. It didn't work. It couldn't work.

Nobody can have two masters, and while she may have spent all of her time diligently doing what her rational mind told her to do, attending to the patients and offering the highest levels of care with a smile on her face, beneath the surface her compulsion to kill was not abating. If anything, having to deny herself the outlet that murder gave her was making things even harder for her. She longed to climb into bed with one of these stupid rich patients and feel them convulse as the life left their body. She hungered for death, and the longer that hunger went unfulfilled the more desperate she became, until finally she could stand it no more.

In short succession, two of her patients passed away. Ostensibly from their existing medical issues, but in reality, from massive opiate overdoses that Jane had administered to them.

If it had been one, then perhaps Jane might have gotten away with it. If she had paced herself, killing one in a month and the other in the next, it would have been lost in the everyday static of death in the hospital, but she got greedy, she saw opportunities to get what she wanted, and she assumed that nobody around her was smart enough to catch her out. Her killings may have started out fueled entirely by egotism before they transformed into some sort of sexual fetish, but it was ego that tripped Jane up, time and time again. She always thought that she was the smartest person in the room and was always surprised when her lies and manipulation were exposed.

Her dismissal from Cambridge probably stung more than her removal from Massachusetts General because it was her 'home turf' and while they too had a reputation to uphold, they made it clear to her that there would be no future for her in public nursing following the deaths of patients under her care. She was responsible for two people dying because of her reckless administration of opiates, and while they did not intend to press charges or make trouble for her, there was no possibility of her finding work in a hospital ever again, and they were willing to make knowledge of her actions public if she pursued another nursing job.

That should have been the end. She should have had no more access to the weak and the sick. The institutions that had shielded her from the repercussions of her actions had turned against her and cast her out. She should not have been able to kill again.

House Bound

Unfortunately for the people of Boston, public nursing was not the only kind. A variety of private nurses were employed all over the city by wealthy families. It was a role and routine that was more than familiar to Jane after all her time with the Toppans, and in a strange way, she welcomed what was for her a return to normalcy. Sleeping with one ear open in case her master called her from her room which was a fraction of the size of those the masters kept. It was a step backwards in terms of her personal freedom, but a step forward in her pursuit of complete control over the lives of others. She was employed by dozens of New England families in the years after her dismissal from Cambridge Hospital. Living in with each family, providing their elderly and sickly with around-the-clock care and forging such documents as were required for her to acquire the medicine that she needed without having to involve any of the hospitals that had such contempt for her. Here in the privacy of their own homes, with no doctors keeping an ever-watchful eye on the nurse, Jane was free to do whatever she wanted to her victims. In the hospital, she had only a limited window in which to act, a few weeks and rarely more before the patient died or recovered. Either way, they slipped through her fingers all too soon. With long-term palliative care right in the homes of her patients, they were completely at her mercy.

While her activities in public hospitals can be, at least partially verified and reconstructed, the events that happened behind the closed doors of private homes cannot.

For five years, through the 1890s, Jane killed. She moved all across New England, and the Boston area specifically, to care for the sick and the elderly in their homes. In her earlier periods of private employment, she was not very discerning about her clients. She was still in a spin after losing her job at the hospital, still trying to find some sort of stability, and latching onto whichever family might offer that. Her clients themselves had little to say for themselves while under her care, as she tended to keep them in a drug-induced haze for the most part, but their families, she pandered to perfectly. Reassuring them that they were doing the right thing for their sickly relative by having her there, providing detailed updates on their health that greatly exceeded any expectations of a nurse, and frequently went beyond what even the doctors had told them. The clients were her victims and playthings, but she treated their families with the utmost care and respect. She earned such a good reputation that the doctors who had no prior knowledge of her before she came to care for their patients began recommending her to their other patients when the time came for long-term care.

Everything kept coming back to reputation. What was known about her was meant to constitute everything that mattered in the world, but what was known of her was more like the tip of an iceberg, with the vast and lethal expanse of reality hidden beneath the surface. Society and their judgement of her status and character were meant to define her but, in fact, they did the exact opposite by allowing much of the truth about her to be hidden from sight for the sake of politeness.

In most cases, when a new member of 'the help' came on board in any upper-class family, they would not only be vetted by the family but by the staff too. Whosoever was the highest ranking among the male servants would sit in judgment over any men brought into the household, and vice versa with the women. Because of her specialisation, Jane typically bypassed any of the usual initial screening processes, but that did not mean that she was entirely safe from scrutiny. Outside of working hours, all of the servants acted as a system of checks and balances on one another. If a maid was seen getting too close with a gentleman about town, she might expect word of it to get back to whoever was next up the chain of command before she could show so much as a glimpse of ankle to her potential suitor. If one of the grooms was going too heavy on the beer in the local tavern, he could expect to come around with a hangover and a butler glowering down at him. In a strange way, each family's servants became a family in itself, often held to far higher moral standards than those of their employers.

At the other end of the spectrum, you faced the problems that Jane had encountered in the Toppan house. When one of 'the help' was close with the family and held herself aloof from the other servants, believing herself to be better than them, that person wouldn't be able to count on support coming from the other servants. It had been one of the reasons that Jane had been so easy to dislodge from the Toppan household. Normally, the other servants would have applied pressure and influence to protect her and keep her around, especially as a servant who had grown up in the household as a part of their under-stairs family, but Jane had been closer to a member of the family upstairs and, as such, nobody made any efforts to cover for her or keep her close.

It was a mistake that she would not make again. The other servants in the houses where she served as a private nurse might have been initially taken aback by her arrival, and the sterile and severe manner in which she handled business, but they soon warmed to her once she had unveiled the lower-class personality that she had been holding in reserve all this time. The daughter of a drunken lout, known as Jolly Jane for her japes and humour, found herself not as an ostracised outsider amongst the help in the houses where she stayed, but as a sort of matriarch to the other servants. When her work was done upstairs, she'd take the young ones out for a beer, or if they needed to stay close, crack one open at the kitchen table downstairs. She may have been educated and demure for the masters, but down among the common folk, she was a ribald drunk, her cackles echoing throughout the lower sections of the house.

Servants were, for the most part, pretty straightforward people from a common background and they took well to the new addition to their homes. For them, it was like discovering a saucy old auntie somewhere up the family tree. She had stories from her work all over the place, along with a vast catalogue of other stories that probably weren't true but were equally entertaining. She got to know people with a casual ease as if there was never a doubt in her mind about social rejection or awkwardness. It went beyond mere confidence and became almost a reality-warping effect, where everyone simply accepted that she had always been there and always would be. As it turned out, all that Jolly Jane had ever needed was that little bit of extra confidence that came from holding life and death in her hand every single day.

The simplicity of the other servants in comparison to the clandestine hoops and loops that had to be leapt through upstairs made the experience quite a relaxing one for Jane. Manipulations that would have been immediately shot down upstairs worked down here on the people who weren't familiar with them. Among the servants of the world, the kind of social manipulation and game-playing that were common in the upper half of the world were essentially unheard of, and would, for the most part, have been completely ineffective, but with crass jokes and off-hand comments Jane soon had everyone dancing to her tune. And of course, anyone who didn't like her, who didn't appreciate bawdy humour and beer-swilling nursemaids soon found themselves on the outs with their colleagues and employers with impressive rapidity.

The social network of the upper class was striated and siloed, complex alliances and wars were fought between the various families of New England completely unseen by normal people, and this inevitably led to Jane being cut off from vast swathes of potential victims by the battle lines that had been drawn between the various segments. Not so under the stairs. Servants of different households had far more in common with one another than they had any allegiance to their masters, so when a trusted servant in one house was asked to seek out a nurse to join the roster, Jane now had access.

Finding new clients was usually not the biggest part of a private nurse's job, given that their entire purpose was to ensure the longevity of their current client and therefore their contract of employment, but Jane always had one eye open for the next big job. If an opportunity arose, she never had to deal with the awkwardness of leaving a job early with her current employer left in the lurch for care, because she had her exit strategy down to a fine art.

All of this is not to say that Jane had no issues at all during her tenure as a private nurse, there were obviously families who were surprised to see their beloved relatives slipping into rapid decline under her care, never quite dying but never quite getting better either, but more pressingly, there were the thefts.

Despite the quite reasonable rate that she commanded for her services, Jane always wanted more. She drank a fair portion of what others would have saved and had been raised in two households where the concept of savings were alien. One, because there was never going to be a moment that they'd rise above poverty long enough not to spend every penny that they made, and the other that had so much generational wealth that earning an income was seen merely as a secondary side effect of employment, with the primary requirement of any job being the esteem it granted. With this in mind, she was always on the lookout for any odd cash or valuables left lying around that she believed that she could get away with taking. Time and time again, suspicion would fall on her. Sometimes she could manipulate things behind the scenes to ensure that another member of the household staff took the fall, and sometimes she could ensure that the patient that she was meant to be caring for was in such crisis at the moment her robbery was noticed that all attention was turned away from such petty matters. Rumours did begin to spread that she had sticky fingers, and that closed some doors to her moving forward, but she already had such a vast potential client base that she could simply pick and choose from among those who had never heard such rumours.

More importantly, she began choosing her clients more and more for their isolation, rather than any promised increase in pay or particularly extravagant circumstances. Her interest was not in prestige, but in performing her duties, and taking her pleasure, without being interrupted by meddling maids or interfering relatives. There were many houses that she went to in the later part of her career as a private nurse that would have been best described as being 'in decline.' Families that had once been powerful and wealthy but now had come upon hard times. Houses where there were no other staff, and she had to see to the cooking and cleaning for herself, as well as nursing the client. Most nurses would have baulked at such a role, given their background, but Jane had spent most of her early life as a maid, and she saw no reason not to take advantage of that. She felt no shame in it, even though she probably should have because it gave her the one thing that she wanted more than money and station. It gave her power. She had complete control over everything that happened in the homes of these sick and elderly victims. They could not sleep or wake without her say-so. They couldn't use the bathroom alone or feed themselves. Every aspect of their life was reliant on her grace, and if she chose to withhold that grace there was nobody around to bear witness to the cruelty that she was inflicting, and the patients were typically too drugged or poisoned to even have an awareness of what had happened to them.

So began a phase in Jane's life where she was actively working to save lives rather than end them. Going above and beyond the call of duty time and time again to keep the clients alive so that she could continue enjoying their largess. With one catatonic patient and a whole house to herself, she was living a life of luxury that she could never have expected in her wildest dreams. But dream she did, dressing up in old ballgowns and flouncing around houses bigger than the whole apartment building where she'd lived as a child. Swilling wines of ideal vintage along with her nightly beers and imagining what life could have been like if she had been born to this instead of the nightmare that she actually arrived in. Wondering how life would have been if she and her step-sister had their roles reversed.

To say that she was living the good life at her client's expense would greatly underplay what she was doing. She wasn't living the good life; she was living their lives. She was pushing them into drug-induced comas and stealing their lives. Their homes became her home. Their wealth, what little of it was left, became hers to squander while maintaining them for as long as possible on death's door. Until now, the joy of toying with her patients had been sufficient to incentivise everything that Jane had done, but now there was a massive lifestyle incentive too. So long as they lived, she lived in the lap of luxury.

The entire purpose of hiring someone like Jane was to ensure that the person she was caring for didn't need to be thought about again. A small expenditure ensured their ongoing survival, for so long as they were liable to survive, and any potential guilt that might have arisen from abandoning a sick or elderly relative vanished into thin air. As such, the number of times that someone would drop by to check in on her patients were few and far between. Examination of the patient's physical condition would confirm that they were wasting away on schedule and were in the kind of mental decline that there was no coming back from, and when they did finally pass away in

Jane's embrace, there would be no question of what had befallen them. Old age and sickness were what brought Jane into their households, and old age and sickness were her accomplices and her alibis.

Yet there were still occasions when relatives made the journey to the town and wanted to drop by to visit with some elderly aunt or uncle, putting Jane ever so briefly in the spotlight. None of these went so badly that she was ever let go from a position, but almost every one of them seemed to come with a decline in opinion about her. The house that was meant to have a full complement of staff to keep it clean wasn't as spotless as the visitors might have liked. The more expensive of the furnishings may have been mothballed or vanished entirely. It was never enough for an accusation to be made, but it was more than enough to temper any goodwill towards Jane, and often to remind the visitors of rumours that they'd heard of nurses committing petty theft against the people they were meant to care for. Admiration and respect soon devolved into contempt as families realised that there was essentially a stranger living in one of their properties, and living well, while the person that they were meant to be caring for showed no sign of improvement.

The almost romantic notion of a servant being adopted into the upper-class family that they served never came around for Jane again, and slowly but surely, she banked enough money that her need for clientele became less about making ends meet, and more about indulging herself. Both in terms of the higher standard of living she could have as a parasite suckling on the underbelly of these wealthy families, and the pleasure that she could take from culling their sickly and weak.

She took up residence in a rented apartment after the end of one longstanding engagement, with plans to rest a little before picking out a new client. Her landlord, Israel Dunham, lived with his wife just next door, and the three shared a convivial relationship, even if the man did sometimes worry that Jane's constant drinking was liable to result in her being unable to pay her rent.

During this period, Jane would begin seeing suitors again for the first time in her adult life, some of them married, some of them available, but there was a constant theme of desperation throughout her attempts. While living in with clients, she obviously couldn't go out courting, so she now behaved as if she had to squeeze all the years that she'd missed into a few short months. If the Dunhams heard anything untoward happening through the paper-thin walls of their apartment, they never mentioned it to anyone, but there were plenty of raised eyebrows regarding all the gentleman callers that came by looking for Jane. It was here, again, that we saw some of her true talents shine as she aimed for personal gain in a new arena. With carefully designed dosages of various poisons and drugs, she could sicken and heal her suitors and herself as she saw fit to try and further inflame passions and sympathies. She would elicit gratitude from some suitors by nursing them back to health after inflicting some noxious cocktail on them. Others would come away pale with worry after calling on her and seeing how sickly she herself had become, only to experience a rush of euphoria on seeing her return soon after, as hale and hearty as she had ever been. Manipulation had always been one of her hobbies, but in the pursuit of a husband she had stepped up her game in many aspects.

This sudden change in attitude towards marriage came as she entered her forties and realised that everyone she knew was settled down and wed. She had never given much thought to the future as she was growing up, probably because the majority of the time she had been walking on eggshells, just trying to ensure that she survived the week. But now that she had managed to claw her way to a semblance of stability, matters were different. She spent all of her time with the elderly and the dying. People who had nobody that cared enough about them to take proper care of them as they slipped into decline. She had a front-row seat to what her own future held, but with the important caveat that her own descent into misery and ineptitude would be conducted with only a fraction of the wealth that those who hired her had available to ensure a minimum of misery. Without a husband, children, and an extended family to take care of her, Jane was liable to end up back in some poorhouse, treated with all the affection one might offer to a bloated and decaying rat.

Doctors who had once tried to court her and were shot down with a laugh now found that they were being given serious consideration and attention. Something that frequently proved awkward, given that the majority of them had moved on with their lives and found wives in the interim. On the other end of the socio-economic spectrum were the butlers and grooms that she'd encountered in her time bouncing from one wealthy house to the next. Many of them were her friends and drinking buddies, but none of them really saw her as wife material. Throughout the whole process, she told increasingly outrageous lies, mostly for her own amusement, though a common thread seemed to be explaining away all her time in private service by saying that she had been abroad serving as the Tsar of Russia's personal nurse since the last time that she had crossed paths with each suitor. It seemed entirely plausible to the servants she spoke to, given the circles that she had moved in, in New England society, but to the doctors who knew a little more about the state of the world beyond the borders of the Commonwealth of Massachusetts, it was a laughable statement that they took to be a joking dismissal of their question rather than a serious explanation.

Yet despite giving it her all, consuming and dosing others with a small pharmacy's worth of medication and reaching out to every viable bachelor that she could reach, it was to no avail. Her attempts to find love were rebuffed at every turn, and whatever hopes she might have had to settle down and live the life of a married woman soon faded. It seemed that she was going to have to take a more aggressive approach if she wished to secure the future that she wanted.

Israel Dunham and his wife were both elderly and while they were almost always friendly and kind towards their new tenant, something about them seemed to rub Jane the wrong way. Perhaps it was simply the fact that she had to give them money every month, just to live somewhere, when usually people were paying her to live with them. They bothered her. They asked too many questions about her life, prying where they had no right to pry, in the same manner of nosy neighbours throughout all of human history who were just trying to be friendly. Still, Jane didn't appreciate it. She didn't appreciate it one bit.

So when Israel took ill and his wife asked Jane to look in on him while she was out getting the groceries, Jane saw the opportunity to put an end to the nuisance that was plaguing her, and she took it.

Friends from nursing school would later recall some of her offhand comments about the elderly, about how much effort seemed to be wasted on keeping them alive. This was reflected in how she spoke of her landlord now, fussy and feeble. Old and cranky. Not worth keeping around. She ended up watching over Israel more and more often as his health worsened, an absolute blessing for his wife who otherwise wouldn't have been able to cope with it all. Sadly, in spite of having one of the best nurses in the state on hand, it seemed that there was nothing that would save the old man from the inevitable. Even as Jane continued to care for him and do everything in her power to keep him comfortable, he seemed to slip away with terrible slowness.

To Jane's great annoyance, her landlady took over the collection of the rent without any pause whatsoever and somehow became even more of an invasive nuisance than before. Because of the way Jane had helped to care for her husband in his final months, the old woman considered her tenant to be part of the family, or possibly some sort of saint. At the very least, she considered Jane to be the dearest of friends. This led to her spending more and more time with the nurse, and then, oddly enough, to her own health beginning to decline in precisely the same way as her husband's. If not for how suddenly this change had come on, it may very well have escaped notice entirely, but because Jane went from poisoning one of the couples straight to the other, there was some suspicion lingering. Yet the very idea that there might have been anything wrong in the Dunham house was soon set aside. After all, it wasn't as though Israel or his wife could have been poisoned by bad food or a leaky pipe without that clever nurse of theirs catching on. They had the best healthcare anyone in their position could have asked for, and if the sickness was still taking them, then that must have just meant that death was inevitable. Jane eased the two of them slowly from their seats in the common room by the front door where they listened to the comings and goings of all their tenants and into their beds, then on a little further into their graves. Two otherwise healthy individuals were dead, and the only "doctor" to have seen them throughout was some nurse neighbour.

But even if it were suspicious, even if the police were to have gotten involved, the sad truth was that forensic medicine was not so advanced in those years that anything was liable to be spotted. Jane used a variety of poisons and medicines in her lethal cocktails, and the vast majority would have been entirely undetectable by the time that the Dunhams found their way to the autopsy slab. If someone was determined, and ran a full suite of tests, then perhaps some hint as to the cause of their demise might have been discovered, but suspicions just weren't running that high yet.

Ownership of the apartment did not pass to Jane as she inexplicably seemed to expect, but instead to the bank that the late Dunhams had owed money to. Jane found herself being evicted as the building was prepared for sale, all of the hard work that she'd put into making this place a peaceful home without any unwanted interruptions had been completely wasted. This was destined to be only a brief stopover, not a place that she could call home. Not a place that she could put down the roots that she so desperately wanted.

For the next four years, she was back to temporary stays in rooming houses as she tried to line up new live-in clients. Bouncing around, never finding anywhere that felt like home. She continued to quietly indulge her wicked habits as best she could, continued to attempt courting despite no man wanting her, continued to spiral ever lower in her moods as all of her hard work brought her no closer to the sense of stability that she so desperately craved. All of her life had been spent on quicksand, one wrong move away from everything coming apart at the seams and now as she grew older, she wanted solid ground beneath her more than anything. She was even willing to give up her worst excesses if it meant that she no longer had to worry about the world falling away beneath her feet. The clients lived, and she lived vicariously through them, dawdling in their homes, sleeping in their beds, eating the fine food that was meant for them, and it came to taste like ashes in her mouth because she knew it to all be a lie.

After dispensing with a woman by the name of Mary McLear, Jane discovered that she had run out of work prospects for the time being. There were too many rumours circulating about her. Ironically, not rumours that she was massacring the elderly and infirm, but rather that money tended to go missing around her. She needed some time away from her industry of choice to lay low.

With very few opportunities available to her in Cambridge, Jane latched onto the idea that one of her close friends, a cook that she'd met while working in some well-to-do house, would be able to get her a job working in Saint John's Theological College, but there were no positions currently available. Luckily enough though, Jane knew one member of their staff who was soon going to be departing. Her old friend died choking and grasping at her own neck as the strychnine that Jane had poured into her beer while she was distracted took hold.

The job working in Saint John's as dinner matron was hers as soon as she asked for it, thanks to the long and elaborate backstory she had concocted for herself. One might have expected that with all of the lies she told, she would have been immediately caught out and lost her job, but she was more than smart and capable enough to pick it up as she went and make herself look like an expert. She mishandled the money quite frequently so that she could pocket some extra change, and some complaints were made about her overcharging, but none of it ever really came to anything. It was only when she grew bored of the job and let her standards lapse that they were eventually able to be rid of her, and by then enough time had passed that she was ready for the next nursing client.

Return of the Cuckoo

It would not be until 1899 that Jane finally found some idea to anchor her. Or some fantasy too profoundly pleasing for her to leave it alone. She had spent her childhood as the mirror to Elizabeth. She was a commoner of low birth, while Elizabeth was considered to have the bluest of blood. She was a servant, while Elizabeth was the master. She was stocky and thick, whereas Elizabeth was slender and elegant. And Elizabeth, through it all, was everything that Jane wanted to be. She had been playing at living the lives of the wealthy and powerful, but now she wanted the games to end. She wanted to have Elizabeth's life. She wanted to be her so badly that there were times she woke up from the dream of Elizabeth's life with tears streaming down her face. It wasn't fair. But for an accident of birth, she could have been Elizabeth. She should have been Elizabeth. That bitch got lucky, she got everything, the world served up on a silver platter, money, talent, a family who loved her and that would keep and honour her into her decrepitude. And Jane, who had done all the work, who had laboured and risked her life in caring for the girl, her reward was destitution and decay. It wasn't right.

Like one of her dead mother's fairy stories, they were like changelings, swapped at birth. Elizabeth should have lived this life of late nights, aching arms and changing the nappies of hags. Jane should have had the dinner parties and the rich husband and the music playing throughout the house. She'd been robbed of it. Replaced.

Despite their falling out, Elizabeth had always kept an open door for Jane. She had recognised in the other woman a frailty well hidden from the world, and it was her nature to confront the weakness of others with kindness. She knew that their fights had been born of Jane's jealousy over the difference in their situations and her own desire to stay close to her step-sister, and she did not begrudge the woman her upset. In truth, she was surprised that they'd managed to struggle through all the years of friendship that they had given the difference in their stations and all of the other forces working to tear them apart. But because of that, she was unwilling to give up. They had made it through so much, surely, they could survive a few small disagreements.

Yet despite having so much in her life, Elizabeth was still suffering ill effects of her own childhood ailments and the unfortunate cost of having a husband married for the station was a marriage that felt altogether loveless to her on most nights. By the midpoint of 1899, Elizabeth had begun to sink into a depression that concerned all of her friends, family and servants, and a letter was sent to her beloved Jane, asking if she might countenance setting aside their differences in the face of such adversity.

Jane wrote back swiftly upon hearing about her beloved sister's brush with melancholy. She was holidaying down the cape, near a place called Buzzard's Bay, and she would be utterly delighted if Elizabeth might like to come down and spend some time with her on the beach, soaking up the sun and reminiscing over better times. It was precisely the kind of cure that a doctor might have prescribed a depressive woman at the time but offered up instead by a woman that Elizabeth still considered to be one of her closest friends. Everyone was delighted when she set off down the cape to meet with Jane, and Elizabeth herself was spotted smiling for the first time in so long as anyone could remember.

The smiles wouldn't last for long.

Arriving at her own boarding house, she soon joined Jane for a constitutional on the beach and a picnic. The dishes on display were cold corned beef, some locally made taffy and some bottled mineral water that had been laced with strychnine.

All of their lives, there had been an imbalance between them, even though nothing was ever said, they both knew that Elizabeth had all of the power, she could do anything and say anything, and Jane had no choice but to accept it as her due. Now their positions were changing, now Jane was the one with the power, the one who decided which of them left and which of them stayed. As Elizabeth began to cough and splutter, Jane moved swiftly to her side, seizing tight hold of her, running her hands up and down the woman that she'd once called sister and shuddering with pleasure. She could feel the coughs wracking her body, she could feel the slowing of her pulse, she could see as the colour faded from Elizabeth's cheeks and her eyes became glassy. Dragging the other woman into her lap, Jane cradled her. Cradled her like she had when they were both tiny girls, and it was her duty to care for her step-sister through whatever sickness she suffered. Tracing her fingers down Elizabeth's face like she was trying to memorise it. Embracing her tightly as the life began to leave her body. With every gasp of Elizabeth, Jane became more excited and entranced, until finally they reached that final breath, and Jane shuddered with pleasure. It was done.

All of her life, Jane had been incomplete. Half of her heart stolen away by someone else. There had been many who thought it was the suitor who'd abandoned her as a girl, but the truth was that it had always been Elizabeth. Elizabeth who she had given everything to. Elizabeth, the altar on which she had sacrificed her childhood. The other woman had been more than just her reflection, she had been her whole world for so much of her life that just the thought of living in a world without her in it left Jane feeling off-balance. But she had done it all the same. She knew that there could only ever be one Elizabeth in the world, and she was tired of it being someone else.

Elizabeth was everything that she wanted to be. Had everything she wanted. If Jane could have carved off her skin and worn Elizabeth as a suit for the rest of her life then that is precisely what she would have done. It went beyond envy and into the depths of depravity and obsession. This girl, who had treated her like a sister, who had fought for her, every day of her life, every step that she took, who had been Jane's mirror to see what the perfect form of herself might look like, she was gone. Jane had killed her. She had felt the life leaving Elizabeth's body. Felt the incredible pleasure as she ripped that beautiful and perfect soul free of its mortal shell.

At once, word was sent to the doctor of the town, to the family of the deceased and all the rest. Jane rode back into the city beside Elizabeth, still holding her cold dead hand as the train car rocked. She could scarcely be parted from her step-sister throughout all of the funeral preparations, right up until the moment that Elizabeth was finally lowered into the rich earth of New England. Then she returned home with the family.

She stayed with them for a week or so, with the family that she had been cast out for. Oramel Brigham, the man that Elizabeth had married all of those years ago was kindly towards his dead wife's friend. Treating her as Elizabeth would have wanted her treated, like a sister. But her intentions towards the upstanding and church-going man were anything but sisterly. When he put a kindly arm around her to try and offer comfort, she flung herself against him. When he tried to disentangle himself from her, she pressed her lips to his. He was mortified, both at how grotesquely forward Jane was being, and with the very idea that a day after his wife was buried he might make off with her sister. The whole thing disgusted him. But still, politeness was the law of the land, and politeness dictated that in times of crisis, people would act out and be forgiven without question. Despite her annoyance at the failure of this seduction, Jane had the good sense to make her apologies for it immediately, explaining that she was overwrought with emotion.

That night she lay alone in bed seething over her failure. It made no sense. He had loved Elizabeth, had wanted her, had kissed her with the kind of wild abandon that would have made most men of the period embarrassed, but now here Elizabeth was again and he had no interest. He was not being taken in by the changeling. She had thought that moving quickly would have worked best, slipping into the empty hole in his life that Elizabeth had left before it could begin to close, letting it heal around her, so she ended up locked in his affections with all the same passion that he had felt for her victim-sister. But it seemed that more effort would be required. The hurt in his heart was still too fresh for her to touch it, let alone press herself carefully into the shape of it. She needed a fresh approach. She had to build a rapport of her own with him. The only trouble was, she had no idea how to do that. Her natural charms were apparently being overlooked, so she'd have to find some other way to win him over like she had, so many suitors before.

By morning, she had composed a plan that was sure to win the heart of any man and set it into motion. The Brigham family had just been rocked by an untimely death. The beloved mistress of the house fell to an unexpected and unexplained apoplexy. The death of their cook was a very minor tragedy, by comparison, happening so soon on the heels of Elizabeth's passing.

It was precisely the kind of household problem that Oramel had no clue how to manage, the sort of thing that his mother would have dealt with back home, and that his wife would have managed for him now. The running of the household was a woman's work, and without a woman, he felt ever more bereft. The kitchen stove which had stayed lit for years on end was cold the morning after the cook passed in her sleep. As if the other staff had let it die in solidarity with her. With no cook and no stove, Oramel, already lost in his grief, had essentially consigned himself to cheese and hardtack to get him through the day until he could deal with the laborious process of replacing her.

So imagine his surprise when Jane bustled in with a hot bowl of stew and freshly baked bread for him to eat when dinner time came rolling around. She stood and watched him eat. Her usually sour countenance twisted into a smile. A smile that only widened when he repeatedly tried to dismiss her with praise. "Delicious."

She still didn't leave.

"The best I've ever had."

She still didn't leave.

"I believe I could eat this very same stew each day and never tire of it."

Still, she lingered.

Eventually, he made his way through the whole meal under her watchful eye, and he couldn't help but wonder if that hadn't been the point of the audience. He knew offhand that he had not been taking the best care of himself since Elizabeth's funeral, and he couldn't help but feel like Jane was trying to do right by him and keep him healthy.

This was not the case. His health and mental well-being meant essentially nothing to Jane. Her interest was in something else entirely. She was convinced that she was an exceptionally good cook and hoped that she might win his heart by showing off her virtues and assets in a more flattering light. They said that the best way to a man's heart was through his stomach, and over the years, Jane had borne witness time and again to how much social cachet a particularly good cook received. In all her years in service, she had not encountered a single household cook who was not happily married, often with a dozen children to boot. Something about eating a woman's cooking made a man fall for her, and she meant to make the most of that mysterious benefit.

Come morning, she made the scandalous choice to come into the master suite alone with a breakfast tray that she'd made up herself. Still lost in his grief, Oramel didn't even realise what was happening until she was standing over him, that same gormless smile plastered all over her face.

All throughout the day, each time that a meal approached, so too did Jane with a tray in hand. He remained courteous to her and he was, in his own way, grateful to her for picking up the slack but at no point would he have construed such a thing as being flirtatious. If he had thought of it that way he would have put an immediate stop to it. He had a problem, and the women around him were rallying to fix it, as was good and proper. But cooking certainly didn't win him over to loving his 'sister-in-law.' In truth, he could barely stand the woman, as polite as he was to her. She was a reminder of his wife's death. A nurse who inexplicably hadn't done a thing to help when his sweet Elizabeth's body was wracked with illness. A doughy-faced commoner who he wouldn't have wasted the time of day on, if not for her connection to his deceased wife.

Jane believed that she was exhibiting the qualities of a good wife without realizing that this was a man who had grown up so privileged that the idea of a wife having to cook for herself was alien. To him, it was the duty of a servant, and he found the whole thing to be intensely confusing. Here was this woman, treated by his wife as though she were an equal despite the massive difference in their stations, and now Elizabeth was gone and he was left with her. He had no connection to her, no understanding of her, and no way to make sense of her relationship with his wife, her relationship with him, or where she fit into the hierarchical worldview that he inhabited. Was she a servant or a guest? Was she his wife's sister, or her maid? Manners would dictate that the way he treated her would be entirely different depending on which of these roles she was meant to fill. He had been treating her with all the kindness of a sister-in-law before, but now it seemed she had made the jump back over the fence into the servants' quarters and wished to work for him, preparing meals instead. The whole thing just served to make him ever more confused about her, on top of his already existing confusion over her long absence from Elizabeth's life which had begun more or less simultaneously with their marriage. Of course, on top of everything else was his confusion about why this extremely forward woman was flirting with him so gregariously when the pair of them were meant to be sharing the communal bond of loss.

The more that she tried to prove herself a worthy wife to him, the more he viewed her as a servant, and therefore not marriage material. What would have served as courtship in the lower and middle classes instead served the opposite purpose here, driving an even greater wedge between the two of them.

It would take Jane almost a week to realise that cooking was not going to win him over, so she abandoned her duties just a scant few days before a new cook could be brought on board. That had been her first plan, reflecting what she'd been told by her nursing friends about the nature of romance. Now it was time for her to switch tactics to something that she was more familiar with.

She had won her way into Elizabeth's heart by nursing her and nurturing her through a bout of terrible illness. It had been the first bond that she had ever truly made, and in a strange way, Jane felt as though she were honouring her sister now, as she slipped poison into Oramel's food before bringing the tray to him.

The dosage was small at first, just enough to make him feel unwell without any obvious symptoms being displayed, but from there, it did not take long to escalate. To make him too weak to function without care and assistance. To pin him down in his bed with nothing but a drop of clear liquid added to the broth she was spoon-feeding him.

It seemed, for a time, that death had come to roost in the Brigham House. Taking first the wife, then the cook, and now looming overhead like a circling vulture, staring down at the man of the house. Yet as close as Jane kept on summoning that looming death, there was no moment when she lost composure or control. She took Oramel Brigham to hell and back, keeping him teetering on the line between life and death, until she felt certain that he must have been entirely overwhelmed with gratitude towards her for the kindnesses that she had done. Only then did the dosage abate and his health return. And even then, only ever so slowly.

Gratitude was not the right word for what Oramel felt towards Jane now, it was an obligation. He had tolerated her presence in his home at first out of social obligation, but as she had asserted herself more and more as a member of the servants, he had begun to feel more and more justified in finally demanding that she remove herself from his home. Now all of that progress had been entirely set back, as he listened to stories from his staff about the time when he was lost to fever and sickness and Jane had stayed by his side, nursing him back to health. She had even slept in the same room with him, night after night to ensure that he was never unattended despite the uncomfortable fact that it might have called her virtue into question. Oramel couldn't besmirch the name of the woman who'd tended him so vigilantly by saying that he didn't think she cared much for propriety, so he had to pretend that the risk to her reputation was real and that she had in fact sacrificed much to be with him in his hour of need.

The staff were actually most impressed with Jane's handling of the whole matter. Whatever else she might have been, harlot, poisoner or anything else, she was above all competent when it came to the care of her patients. She could not have kept so many of them lingering on the border of death if she weren't so very competent. While many of them had been put out by the woman's arrival, and fearful that she was going to try and use her connection to the family to leverage herself into a position of authority under the stairs, especially when she started coming down to use the kitchens after the cook's passing, but the way that she had conducted herself through the master's sickness had removed all doubts about her from their minds.

Such circumstances left it down to the two of them which direction their relationship would go. The disparity between them had been removed by the self-sacrifice and kindness that Jane had shown, and in a way, she had damaged her marriageability by caring for him so. There was no telling what had happened behind closed doors on the long nights she had waited on him, and that meant that there could be no certainty that any suitor might look upon her as virtuous. The direction of social pressure had now switched. It might even be viewed as an admission of guilt, or churlish, if he were not to pursue this woman romantically now that she had done so much for him. Yet the unfortunate truth was that he simply held no affection for Jane, despite all of her best efforts. There was nothing appealing about her in his eyes, and though there should have been a close bond between them after all that they'd experienced, he just did not feel it.

As a talented manipulator with many years of experience, Jane believed that she had exactly the solution to this problem. A mirror to how her relationship with Elizabeth had been forged. It was not enough to do things for the man, it created no bond. He had become accustomed to receiving things as his due, and never felt any obligation to return the affection. She'd been through more than enough rough-handed suitors to realise that.

While it seemed contradictory, the thing that she really needed was to create a situation in which Oramel had to do something for her. Preferably an equal kindness to the one that she'd already done him. In so doing, he would feel a certain equity restored between them. He would feel doubly attached to her for having been on both sides of the equation. He would come to realise how much of a chore and challenge she had endured in caring for him, and through the combination of all these things she might secure his affections.

Just as she was reaching the very limits of his patience with her stay in his home, just when they were approaching the point that politeness would allow him to be firm in demanding that she depart, she fell ill.

Just as she had a long history of manipulation, so too did she have a long history of sickening herself using medicines, poisons and other means so as to elicit sympathy from her suitors.

Bedridden with a mysterious sickness, she was laid up in the guest bedroom, and Oramel immediately set the servants to work caring for her and sought out a doctor, regardless of the expense. His own visits to her sick room were few and far between. He quite naturally feared a relapse of his own having not yet fully recovered from the last bout of illness that he'd been through, and he had no intention of exposing himself to impropriety or to danger by lingering at Jane's bedside. It wasn't going to work. Unless he was the one to come in and care for her, they were never going to bond the way that Jane wanted them to. This meant that she had to go on prolonging her illness far beyond her original intention. Surely, given enough time, he would eventually stop in and try to help her as she had so readily done for him. Surely he had enough affection in his heart for her to do that at least.

The doctor arrived to examine Jane and found that her own reporting of her symptoms perfectly matched up to what he had observed, exactly as he should have expected from an experienced and highly trained nurse with such a prestigious background. Unfortunately, neither that reporting nor the symptoms helped him to work out what was actually wrong with her. At first, he assumed that there must have been some sort of strain on her organs that he was unaware of, then he thought that she might have been exposed to something toxic which was wreaking havoc with her innards, but neither made any sense given the longevity of the sickness. In the end, he had to admit defeat and state that she was suffering from some sort of unknown infection.

From there, the illness persisted, never worsening much, never improving much. She lingered there, just ill enough that she had to be waited on hand and foot, but never quite sick enough to get on with it and die. Oramel, of course, wanted her to make a full recovery. The idea of a third death under his roof in quick succession haunted him. Yet in spite of that, he could not help the mounting aggravation that he felt towards the woman. She had come into his home, latched on like a parasite, and just as he'd been ready to brush her off, she'd attached herself right onto the thickest artery she could find. Even though he never saw her, his staff were running after her most of the day. Even though he never spoke to her, she dominated every conversation going on in the household. And the price that the doctor had charged for his visit was just another small number added onto the ever-mounting bill that had long since come due. All throughout her unwanted stay she had drunk his wine, eaten his food and made use of his home as if these things were her own and she was entitled, with nary a please or thank you. And while he had footed the bill without complaint as a man of good manners and breeding, that did not mean that he was oblivious to just how much this stranger had disrupted his life and his household. Her cloying presence had made the period of mourning which should have been entirely about his dear Elizabeth and how he might continue his life without her, entirely about Jane, instead.

This latest bout of illness had been a testament to just how badly she had overstayed her welcome. Oramel couldn't even contemplate the audacity of going to a stranger's house, letting yourself in and then demanding that they care for you afterwards. She should have been long gone before even he had become ill, let alone lingering until she caught something too. It was beyond the pale.

She had tried to make herself the object of his affection by becoming ill, but she had made herself the object of his contempt instead. Each time he visited with her, it was to check on her progress in the desperate hope that soon she might be shucked free of the bed, bedroom and house entirely. He did not want her here. He had never wanted her here. And her attempts to ingratiate herself towards him had only ever done the complete opposite. She remained exclusively because Oramel was too kind a man to cast her out into the street to die. His loathing for her was nearly absolute.

Eventually, even the ever-hopeful Jane had to concede that the plan wasn't working. She'd given her new husband-to-be endless opportunities to rise to the occasion and care for her, and it had become clear that it simply wasn't going to happen. She began lowering her dosages. On the mend gradually, so that it was not too sudden or suspicious, and then finally, months after she had first insinuated her way into the house, she was well again, and nothing was standing between her and the door.

Nothing except for her digging her heels in.

At dinner that same night when she had finally recovered enough strength to dine among company once more rather than being spoon-fed broths, he asked her what her intentions were. Where she intended to find lodgings, and where he could send her luggage. Ever generous, he even offered to have his driver take her to wherever she was headed rather than uncerimoniously booting her out of the door.

Jane looked bereft. "You're casting me aside?"

It took him more than a moment to even grasp her meaning. Then, confused as he'd ever been as to her intentions, he explained that he had never embraced her to begin with, so casting her aside was an impossibility. He had no romantic intentions towards her, nor any interest to that effect, and the fact that she had somehow convinced herself otherwise made the thought of her staying in his home for any longer into an even more concerning and perilous prospect. He wished her well and had given her such assistance as he could, in memory of his beloved Elizabeth, but that was the extent of his obligation to her, and the extent of their relationship. They were not courting, never had been, and even if he were ready to court again so soon after the death of his wife, it would not have been with her.

"Used, and then cast aside." Jane shook her head sorrowfully. "I'd thought better of you, sir."

Once more, he questioned in which manner she supposed that she had been used during her long holiday in his residence, and then found himself startled into silence when her mask of sorrow slipped away to reveal a cold stare beneath. "In the carnal manner, sir."

He leapt to his feet in horror. Not once had the two of them had any longer physical contact than her first attempt at kissing him. There was no stretch of the imagination that might have led her to think that anything improper had gone on. "But that isn't what people are going to think, sir. That isn't what people are going to say. They weren't in your rooms in the dead of night when nobody was around. They weren't in my rooms when you came visiting."

He had done nothing of the sort and made all manner of protestations to that effect while she just sat there and watched him getting worked up. But of course, she was correct. It wouldn't matter whether what she was saying had actually happened or not, he would be hanged, drawn and quartered in the court of public opinion, his reputation in ruins, memories of his sweet Elizabeth forever tainted by the vile idea that he'd bedded her maid in the days after her passing. He denied every part of her claims, barely even having the good sense to recognise blackmail until she started making her demands. A proposal, a wedding, the life that her adoptive sister had enjoyed. She wanted it all, and in exchange, she would keep anyone from knowing his dirty little secret.

He exploded at her that there was no secret to keep, but a knowing smile spread over her face and she laid both hands on her stomach. "They'll know all about it when the baby comes."

There could be no baby because they had never had sex. Even in the deepest chaos of his fever dreams, he would have known if she'd climbed into bed with him. Or so he thought. Was it possible that she had actually...

"Get out! Get out of my home, get out of my life, never darken my door again!" He moved to bodily haul the woman out of her chair when she didn't move.

"Not so rough!" She grinned. "You might hurt the baby."

He snatched his hands back from her, horrified all over again, but in his wrath, he struck upon the solution to the situation entirely by accident. He told her in plain terms that he had loathed her from the moment that he laid eyes on her, that they would never have any sort of relationship, let alone a marriage, and that if Elizabeth knew the vile trick that Jane was trying to pull then she would have been disgusted with her. He didn't care if she ruined his reputation, he didn't care what she said or did, so long as she did it away from him. He never wanted to lay eyes on her again, and if he did, it would only be for so long as it took to summon a policeman and have her arrested. This was blackmail and deceit, she had no baby within her because no matter how crazed by sickness or drugs he had become he would never have laid hands on her because she was disgusting.

Jane's composure finally faltered. The last words stung enough to break through. There was no baby. She admitted that. But it would be oh so easy for her to make one. She didn't need him to put a baby in her, the whole world was full of men desperate for what she had hidden between her legs, and she'd give it to them all. He'd never even know whose bastard was going to inherit his whole estate if he didn't wed her and bed her in swift order.

At last, the realisation came to Oramel. This woman was mad.

Summoning his servants, he explained to them all exactly what had happened here this night, sparing no detail. He then asked them to collect Ms Toppan's belongings from where she had scattered them about the house and deliver them to the front door. There he waited in the hallway, along with Jane, who had now switched back to being cloying and pleading. There was no need for all this, she had misspoken, she had overstepped. He would hear none of it. With her scant belongings packed, she was physically removed from the house.

Somewhat inevitably, Jane abandoned her plan to ruin Oramel Brigham's reputation. To her, the prospect of getting pregnant and carrying a baby to term was too repulsive for her to even contemplate carrying on with the threatened deception.

Family Curse

There are some accounts that claim that Jane attempted suicide at this point in her life, overdosing on a heavy injection of morphine that proved to be less than lethal due to the amount of the substance that she had consumed over the course of her life. However, finding any evidence of this in historical records is difficult. If she did make an attempt on her own life, it may have happened without her ever being admitted to a hospital. Another possibility is that whichever hospital she had been admitted to may have kept her in their care under a false name to protect her reputation. This was not uncommon when a 'friend' of the hospital did something that would have been considered socially taboo or damaging to the reputation of the institution.

Regardless of whether this attempt took place or not, it is clear that this marked a psychological breaking point for Jane. She had placed all her eggs in the proverbial basket of taking over her adoptive sister's life and with the failure of her ploy, her life was now bereft of meaning and purpose. Before, she always had her "mirror self" to look upon as a measure of what she could have been if the circumstances of her birth had been different, but now she had nothing at all. She had lost one of her few solid anchors to reality with the death of Elizabeth.

Back to where she had begun once more, Jane took up lodgings in a cottage in Bourne and did her best to pretend that nothing had happened at all. As if she had not attempted to slaughter, lie and poison her way into her adoptive sister's place. As if she had not just come face to face with one of the greatest psychological crises of her life and emerged from the other side absolutely wracked with confusion and guilt. All that she needed to do was get things back to normal. Get herself back to normal. Get the usual routine going. Find a way to latch onto some other passing rich family and suck them dry for so long as it took her to feel sated again.

She had rented the cottage from the Davis family, but with no income had soon fallen behind in her payments. Typically this would have been cause for concern, but Mattie Davis was a longstanding friend of Jane's and didn't want to disrupt that friendship over something so petty as money. Still, the fact that the woman wasn't paying her rent was a concern to Mattie. She'd never known Jane to be anything less than meticulous with her finances, and the idea that straits had grown so dire that she couldn't even pay the relatively small amount that they were asking for the cottage worried her greatly. She set out from the family home to go and visit with Jane for a week on July 4th, 1901, ostensibly just as a social call, but primarily to make sure that her old friend from her nursing days was still managing all right.

The recent death of Jane's adoptive sister was public knowledge, after all, and even in the worst times in her life, Jane had never spoken ill of that woman enjoying a life of absolute privilege while she herself had to work her fingers to the bone caring for others.

She arrived to find things oddly serene. Mattie had never really visited Jane at home many times, usually encountering her in the kitchen of some well-to-do family that she was working for, and they're always at the heart of a maelstrom of well-natured chaos, drinking, chatter and good cheer. She'd imagined that in her own place, Jane's huge personality would have flooded out to fill the space, but inside the cottage she found it to be oddly austere. Nothing much in the way of creature comforts, nothing much in the way of decoration, if anything it reminded her most of the lodgings that the hospital had provided to its student nurses where things were kept to almost clinical standards of cleanliness and where spartan décor was the norm. That worried her more. She feared that Jane didn't see this as her home, but just as another temporary stop on her journey through life, and she didn't want that for her friend. She wanted Jane to settle here, to be happy and comfortable. She wanted the woman who had lived her life for others to be able to settle down and have something of her own. But she feared that she'd overplayed her hand in offering this place to Jane. That in asking for so little in rent, and never chasing it, she'd shown that the place was a charity. She knew Jane wouldn't take charity. This was a woman who had worked every moment of her life, from when she was little more than a child herself. Of course, she'd reject anything she saw as charity, and she would treat any home she'd been given as temporary if she thought she only had it because of the kindness of others.

Their time together on the first day was spent personably enough. Some part of the old Jane that Mattie had known and loved came to the fore once they began gossiping about what had become of the other nursing students and the doctors who'd chased after them as if their white uniforms had been an advertisement of interest. Mattie's tales of lusty doctors fell off after she'd left the hospital wards, but Jane was able to pick up from there. She happily chattered on about which of their old teachers had been trying to give her further education in later years, and just how many of them had been doing so while supposedly happily married. The scandal was more than enough to make the whole thing entertaining, even if Mattie did suspect that some of Jane's tales might have been stretching the truth ever so slightly.

Regardless, they had a good time, and after another pleasant day when Mattie felt like she could see the signs of depression leaving her friend, she broached the subject of the rent. The moment she mentioned it, she saw Jane freeze as if she'd been struck, her whole personality seemed to pivot. It was exactly as Mattie had feared, by bringing a business interaction into their friendly relationship, she'd soured it. So she was quick to tell Jane that it was nothing to worry about and that they could settle things up again once she was back to work. There was absolutely no pressure.

Stiffly, Jane thanked her for her kindness and generosity. She explained that she expected she'd be picking up a new client any day now, and was simply waiting on the arrangements being made before she could commit to anything.

Mattie cursed herself for even broaching the subject, she should have waited and let Jane talk to her about it herself when she was ready, but she was so tired of having the debt hanging over every conversation that the two of them had, and she'd always been of a mind that clearing the air was the best thing for friends to do. They went on about the rest of that day much as they had the others, but after dinner that night, instead of sitting up by the fire and chatting into the early hours, Mattie had to excuse herself. She was feeling under the weather and felt like an early night and some good rest might be just the thing to set her right.

With dawn came no reprieve. She had grown even more ill over the course of the night, flushed red all over, but not sweating at all, her temperature running high and her heart slowing to a crawl. Mattie was a trained nurse too, she knew what forms sickness tended to take, but in her own symptoms, she could recognise nothing that she knew. In any other circumstances she would have been in an absolute panic, demanding a doctor or the hospital, but she was here in Jane's house, with one of the best nurses who had ever lived, and when she came in to check on her friend when she was late to rise in the morning, Mattie got a first-hand look at just how efficient and effective a nurse Jane really was. From the moment that she realised something was awry, she had a thermometer tucked in Mattie's mouth and was checking all of her vitals. On a pad by the bed, she scribbled out her notes, and then after a few moments of consideration and calculation of Mattie's weight, which she guessed with remarkable accuracy, she went off to fetch her bag and provide some medicine. Two injections into Mattie's arm had her feeling better almost instantly. Though a big part of that was most likely the fact that one of those injections had been morphine, and she was now too high to notice much of anything wrong with her body. It was the other shot that she really should have been concerned with. If she'd been aware enough of what was going on around her, she might have realised that it was atropine and that her symptoms were consistent with atropine poisoning. Not that Jane was so clumsy that she would have given any indication of that to a 'patient' if there were any chance that they had the wherewithal to comment on it, or if they'd ever have any opportunity to talk about it when they left her care.

The mistake that Mattie had made, of course, was asking for the rent money. Jane had such an aversion to paying rent that she'd already killed two people over a paltry sum, and it seemed that nothing had changed in that regard. People paid her money to be placed and do things, she didn't pay them. It ran against the grain, and she would not endure it.

Over the next few days, her condition continued to worsen, until Jane had to send a letter to her family to alert them to how dire things had become. In essence, she explained that Mattie was now beyond the reach of mortal medicine, that she was providing her with palliative care to ease her passing, and that if they had any intention of saying goodbye to the matriarch of their family without needing the use of a spiritualist, now would be the time to come and visit.

All of Mattie's children came rushing to the cottage in Bourne, but her husband could not. Alden Davis was elderly and sickly in his own right, and it was quite within the realm of possibility that going to see his wife pass away would have been enough to carry him over into the afterlife too. Sons, daughters and in-laws came pouring into the humble cottage to lavish sorrow and adoration on Mattie in equal measure, but before their eyes during their many tedious visits, they were able to watch her decline, until finally, still within that first week of arrival, she passed away in the dead of night, with nobody at her side but her dear friend Jane Toppan.

The tragedy rocked the family. They were all utterly distraught by this terrible turn of events, but through it all, Jane Toppan was a rock. The only solid ground that they had to stand on. Someone who had been through all manner of grief and understood the procedures and processes of death in a way that none of them ever could. It was under her guidance that Mattie's body was wrapped up and transported back to the Davis home so that Captain Alden Davis could bid a proper goodbye to his wife and so that she could be laid out in preparation for her burial. Accompanying that grim parcel came Jane. There had been no insinuating herself into proceedings this time. No desire to become involved at all. But she was so central to the death of Mattie, both as her friend and as her carer in her final days, that there was no question of her attending the funeral and no possibility that "no" might be taken as an answer. The entire Davis clan that had descended on her cottage may as well have hoisted her up and carried her off for all the choice that she had in the matter.

They settled in around her in the Davis home in Catumet too, packed so tightly that she could scarcely breathe.

Death, she enjoyed. Being pressed up against Mattie as her final breath rattled in her chest and the scorching heat of the induced fever from the atropine had slowly eased from a roaring fire to a chill had been one of the most pleasurable experiences of her life. But grief, that was another matter entirely.

No matter how much of it she may have created over her lifetime, and how often she had gloated over that which she'd created, to have it pressed right in her face like this was most uncomfortable. She didn't care about these people, or how sad the life that she had taken was making them. She'd done all her own grieving long ago, on the floor of some filthy little apartment with her father stitching his eyes shut in the next room. She considered herself to be above it now. And while she'd had enough practice in her nursing to fake some degree of sorrow, there was always the wall of professionalism to retreat behind. This wasn't just a patient's family, this was the family of a friend, and that family was welcoming her into their aching hearts because she'd been with their mother in her final moments. Completely oblivious to the fact that she was the reason that those were her final moments.

The days until the burial were usually a source of unease for Jane following any killing. The brief window of opportunity during which a competent medical examiner might find something amiss with the corpse that she'd made. But this time they were uncomfortable for entirely different reasons. All of Mattie's daughters clung to her as if she was their mother. As if some remnant of the woman who died remained in Jane. For all that she'd fought and strived to steal her sister's life, to become a mother and matriarch in her own right, she found the experience of it horrifying and alien. She was not accustomed to her every moment being observed, her expression read, her every thought and word dissected by a swarm of strangers with the same faces. For all that she'd complain about her loneliness, a life of solitude suited her far better than all this abrasive inclusion.

Even with Mattie dead and in the ground, the family still didn't seem willing to let her loose. They insisted that she stay on at the house. That she slept in the bed that they'd made up for her right next to the master. That she be a part of their life and their grief.

It did not take long for her to find their angle. Captain Alden Davis was an old man now, his health faltering, and Mattie had been his nurse as much as his wife. While they didn't expect Jane to take up any of the duties of the wife in the household, they did still need someone to care for the Captain, and since she already owed them so much it only seemed fair that she might offer up her services. The last part wasn't stated outright, but it was certainly implied.

She settled into this familiar role almost immediately after the dirt had hit the coffin. From dawn until dusk she was with Alden, seeing to his every need, monitoring his vital signs and providing him with the kind of care that only one of the best nurses in all of Massachusetts could, but even that didn't seem to be enough for the Davis family. Mattie's daughters still kept on coming around to talk with Jane, asking for advice, seeking comfort in her. She had no idea how to deal with it. She did her best, but it seemed that the advice she'd doled out to maids through the years without a care as to how their pathetic lives ended up didn't completely apply to the lives of these young married women. Mattie had been at the heart of the family, someone that anyone and everyone turned to for advice, and Jane was no fit replacement.

Jane had no wish to replace her. Elizabeth's life had seemed glamorous and perfect. Mattie's was all too real, all too human. There was no handsome husband sweeping her off her feet, there was only the inevitable end of that same story decaying in the bedroom beside hers, creeping closer to death with each passing day. There was no dutiful family caring for her in her dotage, there were just swarms of people, so many people, and she didn't know them or care for them, but they all wanted something from her, every minute of every day they were demanding that she help with this or that, that she give them advice or listen to theirs and she felt as though she might go mad if she couldn't get a little peace and quiet. She'd fought so hard to usurp a position just like this scant months before and now she was confronted with the bitter truth.

Minnie Gordon was the eldest of Mattie's daughters, all grown up and married now, and with a little more maturity than some of the other siblings that Jane had encountered. She recognised that this woman sitting in her mother's chair and doing the things her mother would have done was a different person and that making the same demands on her would have been ridiculous, but she still found that she couldn't stay away. There was something magnetic to her about Jane Toppan, this woman who had moved through a crowd of grieving family without ever letting a single tear slip for one of her dearest friends. Minnie suspected that Jane knew the secret to getting through grief. That she'd borne witness enough times to deaths like these that she knew now how to harden her heart against it. By contrast, Minnie herself was stricken by the passing of her mother, unable to sleep, unable to eat, bereft and beside herself with misery. Her life was falling apart around her, her husband had withdrawn, her children were frightened by her sudden turns from smiling to weeping. She needed whatever secret Jane held. She needed a cure to this sadness.

Jane had the answers that she was seeking, secreted away in the medical bag that she'd carried with her from home. A sedative to help her sleep at night. A little something to get her through the day, to make the pain feel a little more distant. It wasn't anything bad, you were meant to take medicine when you were sick, and just because this sickness was in her heart instead of her body, it didn't mean that treatment wasn't required. She dutifully took everything that was prescribed to her, and Jane felt some measure of relief that at least one of the Davis children had come to her with a problem that she could actually solve. The only trouble was, she kept coming back. Kept asking for more. Jane was hardly light on narcotics in her little bag of tricks, but she had no intention of doling them all out for free and having to find someone to sell her more under the table. As with most of the problems in her life, the solution was obvious, when all that you have is a hammer, every problem looks like a nail. And when all that you have in your medical bag is murder...

On July 29th Minnie was found dead in her bed, less than a month after her mother's demise. There was no obvious explanation for her passing, any more than there had been for her mother, but neither was there any sign that there had been violence done or anything untoward had occurred and so she was laid in state to await burial without the indignity of an autopsy.

Caring for Alden Davis was even more of a chore for Jane than her usual subjects, in no small part because he had a veritable hive of family perpetually surrounding him that meant she couldn't just dope him up and get on with doing as she pleased. She actually had to provide him with the care that was expected of her and might have faced consequences if she slacked. It became increasingly apparent that she had made a mistake in taking on this job, but at least with Captain Davis, there was a very clear and obvious way out.

Three days after his daughter's death, the Captain was seen to suffer some sort of seizure, resulting in him being bedridden for just a few short hours before he expired. All of the relatives who had fully intended to come rushing in and wish him well on his journey to the next life missed their opportunity. His official cause of death, as listed by Jane on the paperwork, was a massive stroke. In truth, the medicine that she'd been dosing him with had been adjusted considerably that day in an attempt to induce exactly the kind of stroke that she had described, but only after she was certain he had been seen hale and healthy earlier in the day. It was only once he was laid out in bed that she had the freedom to inject him with the remainder of the overdose. The sequence of events in the Captain's demise appeared totally consistent with her story of a stroke as the cause of death. For all that she might have been in some sort of death spiral now, killing with a rapidity that was guaranteed to draw attention, some rational part of her mind was still working, still trying to cover up for her and her deranged actions. She was staging the victims so that their deaths might be less obviously related to each other, and to her.

With Alden Davis, head of the household, deceased, she had assumed that her stay would be at an end and that she could return to the solitude of her cottage, which once again she inexplicably assumed that she would inherit ownership of after the passing of the legal owner. But the opportunity to leave did not arrive. The family rushed back in like a tide to seek her comfort, to mouth platitudes to her about how much of a kindness it had been to have her around, taking care of their mother, taking care of their father, taking care of their sister even up until the point of them dying in her care. None of them seemed to recognize the connection between the three deaths with the exception of Alden Davis' sister, Edna Bannister.

As the funeral preparations were made for her brother, Edna kept her eyes locked firmly on the nurse who'd sprung up out of nowhere amidst this cacophony of death. One patient dying in her care would not have been suspicious in the least, especially if it was Alden, who was already halfway through the door of death, but the fact that his wife had gone before him was mystifying, and the fact that his daughter had passed just a few days prior, also while within this strange woman's sphere was obvious cause for alarm. At first, Edna assumed that they had the least competent nurse in all of Christendom under their roof, but even a few cursory conversations with the staff in the house and some of her own contacts in the medical world soon disabused her of this idea. It seemed that Jane Toppan wasn't just a decent nurse but was ranked as one of the most intelligent and competent that it was possible to hire. There were some rumours circulating about her once Edna had dug deep enough, whispers of sticky fingers, inappropriate use of facilities and the like, but nothing that could account for their current situation, and certainly nothing that any working woman might not have accrued over so long a career, even if she were entirely blameless.

The very fact that Mattie had retained a friendship with the woman suggested that she was trustworthy enough, and it seemed unlikely that literally every member of the family was so poor a judge of character that they might have invited some criminal into their home. While there was no question that Jane was of a lower class than the people who now surrounded her and treated her as an equal, the rough edges that one might have expected had all been sanded off in her youth while living among the wealthy. She conducted herself respectably enough, so far as Edna had seen, and while there were some rumours of inappropriate relations between her and myriad suitors over the years, they were hardly in any way applicable to the situation that they were in now. She wasn't suspicious that the woman was attempting to mount the butler, she was suspicious that she'd been so closely involved in multiple sudden deaths. An overview of her professional history as a private nurse turned up a great many deaths, but that was just the nature of the profession. She hadn't been hired to care for healthy people who were expected to live on for decades, and in many cases, it seemed that Jane Toppan's care had actually served to extend the life of her patients many months or even years beyond the doctor's wildest hopes. By all accounts, there was nothing untoward going on. But still, Edna could not shake her suspicions.

Further investigation was clearly required to set her mind at ease, and with all of the avenues into Jane's history turning up little to nothing that she could use beyond some stories that seemed a little unlikely regarding her birth family, that left Edna with only the evidence of her eyes to work with.

While there is no question that Alden was the patriarch of the family, Edna had never attempted to capture the role of the matriarch or to position herself as any sort of authority over the Davis clan. She preferred to live a quiet and Puritan life, giving little attention to the business holdings or family ties that the Davis' had. Even so, her seniority granted her a certain degree of respect, so when she summoned Jane to take afternoon tea with her, there was no question that she would attend. She couldn't reject the overture of friendship without alienating the whole family, and for reasons that neither Jane nor Edna had quite managed to find yet, she was still lingering here among them in the midst of all their terrible tragedies.

Sitting face to face with the woman after having built her up so much in her head, Edna felt quite the fool that day. This was just a nurse. Not the harbinger of death, not some cunning assassin, just an unfortunate woman whose profession constantly pitched her against the ultimate force of nature, death. A conflict that it seemed she had fought hard and well for her entire adult life. She stuck to her plan all the same, teasing out information from Jane, learning the little details that would help to set her mind at ease. Exactly how her brother had passed, what medication he'd been in receipt of, the same details for his wife, his daughter. Every answer that Jane gave her helped to ease her suspicions, to make her believe that this was all just a run of bad luck, rather than anything more sinister. It set her heart at ease.

Unfortunately for Edna, it had entirely the opposite effect on Jane. She knew when she was being suspected, she knew how to give safe answers that would give her persecutor nothing to work with, but that did not mean that she did not feel the weight of suspicion upon her. This woman, this Edna, thought that she knew something about the deaths, and that made her a danger to Jane. There was every possibility that even if she answered every question correctly, Edna might come back again with even more questions, or that she might find someone to corroborate stories with. More pressingly, if this Edna was as suspicious as she seemed, then there was a chance that an autopsy might be ordered on one of Jane's victims, and while Jane was always careful and clever, that didn't mean that the chemicals that she had used would go entirely unobserved by the right medical examiner. It didn't matter how much smarter she was than them, or how diligently she worked to outwit them, there were certain matters that just couldn't be hidden, and ultimately the cause of someone's death was one of those matters. Even if all traces of the drugs were gone, the marks that they'd left on the body in its final moments would have been sufficient to bring trouble down at her door.

Once again, when confronted with a problem, Jane Toppan reached into her bag of tricks and withdrew the only one she had. Murder. While Edna was distracted by one of the servants, Jane dosed her tea with poison. The older woman did not notice, nor did she sicken immediately, it would not be until many hours later as she lay in bed that the poison she had drunk began to take effect. Her strength left her, she could not draw enough air to yell for assistance, and all of her suspicions came flooding back, but all too late. There would be no opportunity for her to tell anyone else about what she suspected about Jane, even though she now had the clearest possible evidence that the woman was poisoning her way through the whole family.

With the number of survivors dwindling, Jane now found the Davis household much more to her liking. She was an honoured guest and the servants dutifully saw to her every need, she ate as she pleased, did as she pleased and had no requirements upon her beyond the social niceties. Another funeral to attend, another round of sobs from all of dearly beloved Edna's friends and family, begging Jane to help them through their time of grief with the same stoicism that she always showed.

Genevieve, the last surviving daughter of Alden and Mattie had lost everyone. Everyone that she might have turned to in this time of grief had become a font of that grief. There were so many dead in so short a time that she suffered night terrors that she would be next, that there was some curse upon her family steadily and heartlessly plucking them all from the tapestry of life. In desperation, she turned to the only real constant throughout all of this chaos. Jane Toppan, the nurse who had attended to all of their dead and dying. She told her of her ceaseless sorrow and anxiety, and Jane, in her infinite benevolence, prescribed for her a few injections to take the worst of it away. She would pass away shortly after receiving Jane's medical attention. Two generations of the same family had been almost entirely annihilated in the course of six short weeks.

Everyone involved was grief-stricken. Everyone involved was numbed and blinded by the impossibility of so much horror in so short a time. But eventually, their senses began to return. Logic had been buried with the first of their dead, and each additional grave seemed to have forced it six feet further underground, but now at last, some of the Davis family began to think.

Way back in the beginning of all this chaos, what must have felt like a year before it ended, Minnie Gordon had died in the prime of her life. Her husband and children had been left behind, bereft and distraught. But now, with Genevieve's passing, her husband recognized a terrible similarity. Two sisters, both hale and healthy just days before suddenly dropping dead out of nowhere? It strained credulity for it to have happened once, but twice... twice was ridiculous. Before they could bury Genevieve's body, he went to her husband and demanded that an autopsy be performed. Both men were heartbroken and lost, and both of them were hardheaded enough to think that the other was the one acting irrationally. Genevieve's husband refused. Minnie had been buried without that desecration, so why should Genevieve have to suffer it on the whim of some man to who he was no longer even related to? All the ties that had bound them were severed with Genevieve's passing. Everything that had held his life together had been cleft. Facing a dead-end and opposition at every turn, Minnie's husband did the only thing that was available to him. He could not force them to examine Genevieve's body and prove that something sinister was afoot, but there was one corpse that he held dominion over. A woman was her husband's property in those days, even in death, so he ordered Minnie's exhumation so that she might be properly examined.

It was a scandal. A morbid curiosity being fulfilled and nothing more. The rest of the family, broken as it was, shunned Minnie's husband for what he was doing to her remains. In the pulpit, the local minister spoke out against him, and the dangerous excesses of selfish grief. Loudest amongst the voices speaking out against this pointless interference with the dead was, of course, Jane Toppan, who took it as an insult to her professionalism that they doubted her word regarding the cause of death. Not to mention the atrocity that would be performed on dear dead Minnie. She told them all in excruciating detail about what the process of autopsy involved. She was intimately familiar from having watched so many of them over the years. The hacking and sawing at bones, the wet slurping sound as an organ was pulled free. Brains on the scales. Eyeballs floating in jars. Every horror that she could concoct to try and put them off the autopsy, she unleashed, but Minnie's husband had made up his mind and was not going to be swayed. Something was going on, and he meant to solve the mystery, even if it did cost him his reputation and the fair-weather affections of what was left of the Davis family.

Yet all of their caterwauling was silenced when the coroner's report came back showing a lethal dose of morphine had been in Minnie's system and likely was the cause of her death. It had been sitting there in her veins ever since, even as the body around it decayed. A signature written on the corpse, marking the murderer as someone in the medical profession.

Everyone's doubts and complaints were immediately erased, Minnie's husband was exonerated of any wrongdoing, Genevieve's body underwent the same examination as her decayed sister, and the same morphine was discovered, alongside a bizarre dose of atropine. Both of the girls had been murdered, and if they went on digging up corpses, there was no doubt in anyone's mind that yet more poison was there to be discovered. Some viper had made its way into their nest, envenoming everyone in reach the moment that their backs were turned, and there was no question as to who that viper was.

Jane Toppan was mysteriously absent from the Davis home when the family came calling this time. She had returned to Boston, so far as the staff had been able to ascertain. Her hasty departure occurred at about the same moment that the first body was undergoing its autopsy.

Clipping the Angel's Wings

It would not be until October 29th 1901 that the police finally caught up to Jolly Jane Toppan. She had not returned to any of her known abodes after her departure from the Davis estate, nor had much in the way of contact with any of her known associates. The cottage she had rented from Mattie Davis lay in a state of abandoned disrepair when the police arrived to search it hoping for some hint at where she might have gone. The land register of the time should have shown where any given person in the city of Boston was staying, but Jane appeared nowhere as either a renter or an owner. Not under the name Jane Toppan, nor under her birth name, which the investigators managed to dig up. It was as though she had vanished entirely. What the police had failed to grasp was that Jane never had any need to rent or buy a home. Why would she, when her clientele provided such things for her? As it turned out, Jane had already procured employment in another Boston home with such ease that the police could scarcely believe it.

Since her departure from Catumet, she had taken up residence as a live-in nurse for yet another sickly client, resuming her life, uninterrupted, as though she had not just slaughtered her way through a whole family line. She had gone from a mass murder spree back to changing out bedpans without so much as a blink. To Jane, they were all one and the same, all just parts of the same activity, she felt no need to switch gears or change her behaviour at all. She just kept her head down and went about her duties, waiting for the trouble to simply blow over. As though mass murder were no greater sin than any other faux pas that she might have committed in the past.

Taken into custody, the police were fully expecting to have a raving lunatic on their hands given what she had done, but they found themselves disturbed to discover that Jane Toppan seemed to be as normal as any woman that they might have met on the streets.

She made it clear to them that she was not insane. She stated as much in very straightforward terms. If they said that she was insane, she was not going to help them, she was not going to talk to them, and they would be getting nowhere. She was sane. If she was sane, then she might serve a sentence in prison and be released, but if she was insane, she would never see the light of day again. She knew this, because neither her father nor sister had ever left the madhouses that they'd been confined to. More importantly, she wanted everyone to know that she was sane so that she would not have to endure the indignities that the mad suffered. She had worked all her life in healthcare, she knew exactly how the mad were treated in the care facilities of that time and she would rather have taken one of her own lethal concoctions than suffer such a fate.. Jane Toppan was sane. She understood the consequences of her actions. She knew the difference between right and wrong. And she had chosen to do things that were wrong because it brought her pleasure, and because it was gainful to her. She had killed people because killing them brought her satisfaction, wealth, and all the other things that people wanted out of life but were too scared to pursue.

This statement left the police stunned into silence for a time, and the job of interviewing her was turned over to someone with more seniority. This individual had the good sense to begin the interview by affirming that he would report everything exactly as she said and make no insinuations as to her mental state one way or the other. The process of her interview was not brief. She had been remanded into their custody on suspicion of the murder of Mattie Davis, Alden Davis, his sister, and two of their daughters. All of whom had been confirmed to have suffered poisoning through the use of drugs, in particular, the coroners had found traces of heavy metals in those victims that could only have been introduced to their systems through poisoning.

Jane was surprised that they'd caught onto that one, she'd always assumed that they'd never test for it, since it was so unusual, but then, she supposed that they would have been testing for everything if they thought it was a murder and not just unfortunate happenstance. In all five cases, she provided the police with details of the precise cocktail of drugs and poisons that she dosed each of the victims with. Some of them in a single lethal injection, or via tainting something that they were drinking, others through a series of applications that slowly built up to be lethal. Despite everything, she wanted the police to know that not only was she sane and rational, but she was also the smartest person in the room. Capable of such feats of medical mastery that they could never even conceive of. She described exactly how each of her medical infusions were applied to the victims, with the timing down to the nearest minute. She had some sort of spreadsheet in her head, tracking all of the details as though she were a nurse doing rounds with a chart in hand.

All of the evidence required to convict her of the five murders that she'd committed against the Davis family was in hand, and they now had a detailed confession. One might have thought that the process of interviewing Jane Toppan was now at an end, but the manner in which she had so casually dispatched her victims was entirely too practised for the police to believe that this was the first time that she had killed. While a few officers were sent out to gather statements and evidence regarding what had happened in Catumet, more had now been sent out to examine Jane's history. Her comings and goings, and the people that she had crossed paths with. She had left a trail of death in her wake, invisible only because she was entirely above suspicion up until this point. But now that someone was actually looking, a very grim picture began to emerge almost instantly. Dead adoptive family. Dead landlords. Everyone who had crossed paths with Jane Toppan had been marked for death. Everyone who had ever been in her way had either moved or been moved.

Gradually the victim list expanded until it encompassed eleven murders in all. Eleven people dead and buried because Jane Toppan had decided that they were worth more to her dead than alive. Eleven bodies that were exhumed and underwent the same toxicology testing as her latest victims only to find precisely the same evidence lying in their veins.

In spite of everything, Jane had looked to the police like some mad woman who'd gone on a killing spree, not the cold and calculating killer that her own words were painting her as. They couldn't believe that she had done all that she was claiming to have done in her own confessions. Each one of the murders had to be substantiated because they knew that no court would take the word of a woman, particularly a criminal, at its face value, even though she was obscenely open about everything.

In the run-up to her trial, she was assigned a lawyer, who in turn sought out the assistance of medical experts to try and overturn her own claims to sanity. She was questioned at great length by some of the best psychiatrists of the time, trying to ascertain what particular part of her psyche had broken to make her act out like this, but the truth was exactly as Jane told it. She was aware of what she was doing, she was aware of the consequences of her own actions, and she was in no way ashamed to admit to the truth now that she felt that lying could no longer offer her any sort of protection. In a strange way, she seemed to feel almost relieved to have been caught so she no longer had reason to keep her secrets. Then, in turn, she seemed to be pleased that the world would finally know what she had done. She was proud of all the killing. Proud to have come upon so many entirely helpless people and taken their lives. Some of her interviewers found this statement in itself to be a testament to her insanity, but others recognised that this was a person who had been underestimated and entirely overlooked throughout her life because of her social class and her gender. This was a person who was now finally able to show the world exactly how much she had been able to accomplish.

It was only later during these interviews that Jane's mental state during the killings was properly delved into. It is only from a few brief comments that we are able to piece together the shape of her pathology. The way that it started out as an ego boost, holding the power of life and death in her hands. How she twisted that into an opportunity for vengeance. How the very act of killing, or of holding people on the precipice of death became sexual to her. The arousal she felt when thinking about murder. The orgasm she reached only through feeling the life leaving her victim's bodies.

Such things were so scandalous at the time that they were not discussed in open court, nor were that particular doctor's findings made available to the prosecution. Just the idea of it was so obscene and twisted that it put even the medical doctors trained in the study of human thought and behaviour into a state of alarm. There was no telling what this kind of knowledge might do to the impressionable public. How many other women might take up murder if they knew it was a way to find release?

It simply could not become public knowledge. It was buried, only to be exhumed years later in medical journals of psychology, and even then, not in the most reputable ones.

With eleven confessions in hand, the prosecution was more than ready to send Jane Toppan to the hangman. Without the obscene details of her psychology in hand, her defence attorney was effectively hamstrung in trying to prove that she was insane, and therefore could not be tried. In a somewhat desperate attempt to gain any sort of upper hand in the upcoming court battle, he asked Jane to prepare a confession exclusively for him, including all of the details of her murders, in her own words, with no interference from the police trying to shape her statements.

What he received is one of the most scandalous documents of the 1900s. In her confession to her lawyer, she provided explicit detail of not only the murders of the eleven victims that she was already being tried for but for a full thirty-one. As with her previous confessions, she provided every single detail that only the killer might know, down to the milligram dosage of each lethal ingredient in her cocktails of death. It would have been enough to doom her in court. Enough to end any hope that he might have had of helping her to avoid execution. Anyone reading it would have known that she was sane and rational, that she had planned out her killings with meticulous detail. Even if that wasn't enough to convince them, there was the emotional impact to consider. A madwoman who had killed some people that she knew was one matter, but they didn't even have words in those days for the kind of killer that Jane really was. The horror of it, the randomness of her victim selection, her methodology, keeping people on the verge of death for weeks or months at a time for her own amusement, it was all too much to bear. Nothing in the account contradicted what Jane had told to the police in equally exacting detail, so her lawyer had no use for it, no compelling reason to have it entered into evidence so that all the world might see it and entirely damn his client, even if it was clear evidence that she deserved to be damned a hundred times over.

The trial began in the summer of 1902 and revolved less around whether or not Jane was responsible for the murders that she had confessed to and more about how culpable she was for her crimes given her mental state. While she absolutely insisted that she was sane, the mere fact of her crimes made it difficult to believe. It was considered impossible for any sane person to have done what she did, therefore almost by definition, anyone who had committed those crimes would be found to be insane by the standards of the court.

In desperation to avoid being consigned to the same asylums that her father and sister had been sent to, Jane took her lawyer aside and insisted that he put her on the stand to make a statement of her own. To prove that she was mentally competent. She believed that if they just heard her speak, then her sanity would be apparent to all. Her lawyer, who was the one campaigning the most vigorously for her to be found insane so that she could avoid execution, believed the opposite to be so. He thought that if she took the stand, just a few minutes of listening to her would be sufficient for any juror to condemn her to the madhouse.

Finally given a chance to speak for herself, Jane unburdened herself entirely. She confessed to all of the killings, gave reasoned and logical explanations for why she committed them, and then, when asked by the prosecution, about all of the others that she was rumoured to have killed, she made the statement that would consign her to both the hospital for the mentally ill, and the history books. "It is my ambition to have killed the most helpless people in all the world."

Nobody sane could harbour such an ambition. To her lawyer's delight and Jane's raging fury, the jurors found her not guilty of her crimes by reason of insanity. She tried to fight free of the guards as she was led away, yelling back at her lawyer that she wanted to appeal the court's decision.

Unfortunately for Jane and her lawyer, there was another player in this game that they had not considered. Not the courts, not the families of the deceased, and not even the prosecution. William Randolph Hearst.

Hearst was a second-generation millionaire who built up a media empire at a time before such things were even considered possible. He owned a whole chain of different newspapers and magazines, and he outsold all of his competitors by focusing less on ethical and balanced journalism, and more on scandal, flashy headlines and the worst excesses that today's media often embraces. Understandably, for a man with no morals, and an obsession with getting the most salacious stories possible into print, he was fixated on Jane Toppan's killing spree. It was exactly the kind of story that made his papers sell. It was the kind of story that careers in his papers could be built from. The sort of thing that would make any new journalist looking to break into the industry more than willing to overlook a few silly things like laws, fair trials, and professionalism. One of Hearst's minions bribed his way into the office of Jane's lawyer, dug his way through all of the files that were being kept on her, and found her fully detailed signed confession. The figurative smoking gun, that proved that not only was she exactly the murderer the prosecution were claiming, but that she was also so much worse.

Hearst took one look at the confession and sent it to the presses. It would be published in full in his papers. Every gruesome detail. Every pertinent point. All of it, in the killer's own words. Needless to say, circulation of his papers went up that day.

The courts filed injunctions against Hearst, made complaints both officially and through back channels, but ultimately the cat was out of the bag and there was no putting it back. There was no undoing what had already been published, and no un-reading what had already been read. The American public had seen Jane's confession, and now trying to get her a fair trial in any sort of appeal would be practically impossible. Any competent lawyer would be able to point to any given juror and point out their existing bias against their client.

The appeal was postponed as alternate arrangements would need to be made, and because the police now had about twenty more charges that they wanted to add to the list.

This produced mixed results. The people that she had killed in the hospitals could never be correctly identified, even when digging through all of the records, because there were simply so many deaths in any given hospital ward at any given time, the majority of them never investigated further because the sickness of the person who had died was presumed the cause. As for all of the private patients that Jane had killed through the years, the police ran into an entirely different set of problems. These were all wealthy, high-society families who did not want to be associated in any way with scandal. They did not want their names to appear in any of Mr Hearst's newspapers, nor for their exhumed dead to be manhandled and photographed. They were entirely antagonistic to the entire process of investigation. In most cases that would not have been an issue, the police could have simply steamrolled ahead without their agreement, but in this particular case, they had a peculiarity of law to deal with.

In life, a person was a person, but at the moment of death, they became an object, assigned as property to their closest family member or an appointee. They would then undergo whatever treatment the person with ownership of them saw fit before being buried. Yet at the point of burial, they did not become public property. They remained under the stewardship of their family, and without that family's specific consent, they could not be disturbed, even in the pursuit of a criminal investigation. Without the support of the families of the dead, there was no way for the police to prove that they had been murdered. It didn't take long before the whole investigation had to be called off due to a lack of investment on the public side of things. Without the bodies, they only had Jane's confession, and she could recant that at any moment she chose. More evidence would have been required to ensure her conviction.

In a somewhat backhanded deal, the prosecution made Jane's lawyer an offer. They wouldn't pursue the other murders if he would agree not to appeal the insanity judgment. It was a bad deal, even if the investigation had not been brought to a screaming halt by the stonewalling of the victims' families, but neither the lawyer nor Jane recognised it as such. To the lawyer's mind, this was the best possible outcome. Jane agreed with whatever her lawyer suggested, more or less entirely withdrawn from reality by this point in proceedings, still imagining that she might serve a few years in prison before walking free and starting over again.

At this point, matters of the court were concluded. On June 23rd, she was found not guilty and committed for life to the State Lunatic Hospital at Taunton.

Her arrival in her new home was not without its problems. There was a massive uproar in the press and public thanks to Hearst's publication which meant that she was dogged by justice enthusiasts who wished to see her lynched and baying swarms of journalists trying to catch a quote from her to slap down as their headline for the day. She had to be taken into the Hospital under armed guard to make sure that she arrived there safely, and even once inside she retained a healthy sense of paranoia, particularly about the nursing staff who were going to be dedicated to her care.

For the first week of her confinement, she would not eat. She would thank the nurses profusely, and push the food around on her tray, but she would not actually consume any of it. The staff began to become concerned about her appetite, and eventually one of them managed to extract the truth from her. She believed that she was going to be poisoned. They were nurses, just like she had been, and they had free access to all manner of terrible chemicals. It would have been so simple for them to add just a little something to her food and ensure that she died in screaming agony, retching up blood. The nurses were appalled at the idea that one of them might do something like that, but to Jane's mind, it would have been entirely appropriate. After all, it is exactly what she would have done if someone came into her care that she didn't care for, and she knew that everyone in the world hated her now.

Eventually, she reached a breaking point where she realised that if she did not eat, she would die even without someone poisoning her, and unlike the immediate death of poisoning, she would die slowly, withering away like one of her patients. Steeling her resolve, she began to eat. With every mouthful, she became more convinced that her earlier concerns had been paranoia. With every meal, she regained a little more of her strength and hearty complexion. After that, she settled into life in the asylum about as comfortably as anyone really could. She was kept off the main wards in a private room, just for safety's sake. Both her safety from the other inmates, some of whom might very well have heard about the kind of person that they were now sharing a living space with, and for the safety of their more helpless patients, who it was entirely possible Jane might have enjoyed doing away with, if given the opportunity.

Beyond the walls of the asylum, the truth about Jane and her activities continued to come out, and Hearst continued to stoke the flames, raising public awareness of her crimes, and paranoia about medical professionals, to the greatest heights possible. Yet while the common, working-class people read about the terrible crimes that Jane had committed with a sort of fascination, Hearst's circulation did not stretch to the upper-class neighbourhoods where her victims had once lived. For them at least, the terrible matter of Jolly Jane Toppan could be put behind them and forgotten about.

The years passed. The media frenzy surrounding Jane moved on, feasting on the corpse of the Spanish-American war, along with dozens of other brutal murders all across the states. Gradually, the monster that had been Jane Toppan was forgotten about, even by those in the asylum whose entire purpose was to keep watch over her. By the time of her death in 1938, at the age of 84, she was considered to be nothing more than a quiet old lady by the staff in attendance, but the older, retired staff painted an entirely different picture. Their picture was one of a woman still so firmly dedicated to her calling in life that she would whisper to them when they came into her room, "Go and get some morphine dearie, we can go out on the ward and have some real fun watching them all die."

ANGEL OF DEATH

A Legacy of Carnage

From her confessions and the supporting evidence, it is easy to conclude that Jane Toppan killed around thirty helpless people, but that number does not account for the vast majority of the time that she was killing. She began to murder as soon as she entered training as a nurse, long before the time period any of her confessions touched on.

In casual conversations during her time in Taunton Insane Hospital, she would admit at various times to different crimes, but when the full sum of them were tallied they far surpassed anything that the legal system knew about. She outright admitted to having poisoned more than a hundred people over the years, but of course, some of those poisonings would not turn out to be lethal. Some were patients that she had simply toyed with, others were the minor poisonings that she used to manipulate events. The housekeeper that she poisoned enough to make her seem like a drunk so that she could charge in and take her job. The suitors that she had sickened so that she could swoop in and care for them. She had even poisoned herself on multiple occasions to suit her needs. From her humble beginnings as the daughter of a part-stitcher and a washerwoman, she had acquired a mastery of pharmaceutical knowledge that was almost unmatched in her time period, not only a theoretical grasp of the chemistry as most doctors of the period managed but also a lifelong practice on human guinea pigs that gave her an insight that far surpassed them.

Because she was born poor, Irish and a woman, society as a whole entirely overlooked her and her value. This contempt was both a blessing and a curse for her. Her rage was unquestionably rooted in the way that the world looked down on her, but on the other hand, she was able to get away with so much for so long simply because she could pass through life invisible as a result of that contempt. Because no one at that time even considered a woman to be capable of murder, she achieved one of the longest-running killing sprees in American history. The world didn't yet know about serial killers, and the few cases that had appeared throughout the years bore no resemblance to Jane and her activities. Men with knives and garottes attacking strangers and the kindly nurse sitting by the bedside of an old woman bore little resemblance to one another.

Her position as a nurse gave her access to an endless supply of victims, the medical expertise required to carry out her murders and a mask of virtue. At this point in history, hospitals were just reaching the transition period when they went from being operated by holy orders to being fully scientific in their application of medicine. Much of the awe and respect that had once been extended towards the nuns that had previously served as nurses was now being passed down to their secular counterparts. These were women who had chosen to sacrifice their own lives and happiness to care for others. Women who had abandoned their natural role as wives and mothers to follow a different path, caring for the sickly and the weak. They were venerated by society as being akin to living saints as a result, and Jane Toppan had used that veneration and assumption of benevolence as the perfect disguise. Wrapping herself up in her Jolly Jane persona, bringing smiles and kindness everywhere that she went and inspiring other nurses to do the same.

She inspired the nurses in her time to be better nurses, to pursue their education and increase their knowledge base, but that isn't where her influence ended. Her historical footprint has mostly been minimised because she was killing long before an interest in serial killers came to the fore, but there can be no denying that she has served as a fundamental archetype for a specific type of serial killer. The angel of mercy serial killer is almost always a woman, almost always a medical professional and almost always uses her position to eliminate the sick and the weak that she deems no longer worthy of life. Sometimes this is justified as an act of kindness, other times as nothing more than the egotistical power-play that it is, but all the same there have been dozens, if not hundreds of others following in Jane Toppan's footsteps throughout history. Treading the same ground as her, even with no prior knowledge of her existence. The prevalence of these types of murderers has spread out to become a building block of pop culture, with the "evil nurse" becoming a trope in literature and film stretching back to the time when Jane was operating. The shock value of such a character is the very same dichotomy that made Jane Toppan so fascinating. A person who has dedicated her life to helping the less fortunate, who on the outside appears kind and saintly, but who is actually driven by dark passions to commit acts of cruelty and even murder upon her patients.

There are some who would argue that Jane Toppan was not only the founder of an archetype of serial killer but was also the first American serial killer in history. She is certainly the earliest killer that we have sufficient documentation on to conclusively prove that she committed the crimes of which she was accused. The exact dates of her conviction and crimes could be argued as earlier than some of what is traditionally called serial killers, but simultaneously, the cultural response to acts of multiple murders was shaped by attitudes of the time. She was considered an insane outlier, just as other serial killers of her time period were, but in generations prior, it is entirely possible that their behaviour would have been entirely overlooked or depending on the time and place of the crimes, even applauded. You only need to glance at medieval history in Europe and Asia to easily identify dozens, if not hundreds of what we would now consider to be serial murderers, and in America's bloody past, during the colonial period and westward expansion, there are more than a few 'gunslinging heroes' who would be judged very differently by today's standards.

While there are various records and documentation detailing some of Jane's crimes, none go the distance towards answering the question of how many victims Jane Toppan actually killed.

Thanks to the reluctance of many families to become involved in the unfolding scandal, we lose any hope of tracking how many of her private clients ended their lives under her kind care. Thanks to the complexity of deciphering which deaths were natural and which were not, we struggled to determine how many of the patients who died under her care in hospital did so as a result of her interfering in their medication. Many hospital records, including death registries, have been lost in the intervening years and many were deliberately obscured at the time to cover her tracks by people once again trying to avoid any sort of negative attention or scandal. People cared so much about propriety back then that they found it preferable to allow a woman to run loose and kill for her own amusement, rather than have her brought to justice and risk all of their own faults and secrets seeing the light of day. Jane was very good at making herself invaluable, making herself everyone's friend, and worming her way into the hearts of families and organisations that then took it upon themselves to protect her so that their own involvement in her crimes, whether from negligence, inaction or sheer ignorance, could be sufficiently obscured.

We also encounter the problem that by the time she was able to speak freely without fear of consequences, having accepted her place would forever be in the asylum, she was on her way into old age, and the precise and calculating mind that had achieved so much evil was beginning to break down. Memories were becoming fuzzy, dates and dosages were blurring together and the faces of her victims were merging into one. By the time she had the opportunity to confess all of her murders, she couldn't even remember them all. Not to mention that there was no shortage of times when she had been recklessly administering medicine to people who happened to die of natural causes at around about the same time, or those that she'd 'saved' with her treatments, only for the complications of the strain that she'd put their body through keeping them on the verge of death to catch up to them years later. Because of the methods that she used to kill, and her victim selection, even in an ideal world of eidetic memory and fully documented complete confessions, it would be impossible to assign an exact number.

What we can work out is the most likely scenario, and after many years of study, criminologists seem to have hit on the number one hundred as a ballpark figure for how many people Jane actually killed. Her conviction was for a tenth of that, her confessions accounted for perhaps a third, but it seems fair to say that one hundred different people who fell under her care were poisoned to death by Jane Toppan.

At one hundred victims, Jane Toppan would not be the most prolific serial killer in the world, though she would have the dubious distinction of being the most prolific serial killer in the United States of America.

However, it was not Jane Toppan's goal to be the most prolific murderer, but the most prolific killer of 'helpless people.' And in this, she has most assuredly won in comparison to her peers. With a growing awareness of the dangers of women like Jane Toppan, and improvements in the systems in place to protect patients, no future Angel of Mercy has been capable of killing nearly so many people before being caught. As the first of her kind ever documented, she had the element of surprise on her side. Everyone that came after and attempted to replicate the same feats found that there had been walls raised to defend the innocent against them.

There is of course no way to ultimately substantiate the numbers involved. Even those murders that she confessed to were never fully investigated, only the ones for which she was convicted can be entirely guaranteed to be hers, and even they come with the caveat that at least a few of those people were already suffering from various other health conditions that might have been the ultimate cause of their demise rather than her intervention. One hundred people might have died at Jane Toppan's hands, as experts on the subject suspect, or only a handful might have. The passage of time, and the limited investigative technology available during Jane's time, has robbed us of any hope of real clarity.

Using a combination of drugs that were available to her as a nurse, and a variety of readily available chemicals that could be purchased over the counter, Jane Toppan killed about one hundred people in the span of her lifetime. Killing anyone that got in the way of her plans, killing anyone that she crossed paths with that she thought might suspect her, killing indiscriminately, over and over again, just because the potential victim had come into reach.

But while it is easy to get bogged down in arguments over just how many people she killed, what methods she used to achieve her goals and to avoid detection, how she managed to circumvent such protections as were in place to prevent people from accessing dangerous pharmaceuticals and poisons and other such minutiae, the more interesting question is not how she did what she did, or how many people she did it to. The interesting question is why?

Given the state of psychiatry at the time of her arrest, there are liable to be a great many clues as to the answer of why she did what she did that are as lost to us as the full list of her victims. Likewise, it is quite likely that the police of that era, with their own preconceived notions about what a woman was, what a woman was capable of, and the nature of criminality, have provided us with an incomplete picture of Jolly Jane Toppan's actual statements. But even so, there are many causes that people point to for her murder spree.

The first is the practical. A common trait in female murderers, and poisoners in particular, is that while a man may commit these crimes for passion, a woman will typically kill for a purpose. To remove a threat, to improve her station in life, or to change the world to one slightly more to her liking. The poisoner typically kills someone close to them, more often than not her abusive husband or something similar. For all of Jane's intellect and training, she was ultimately still a poisoner, so it is quite easy to look at her crimes through this lens. The murders that she committed while employed in the hospital could be viewed as her reducing her workload or proving her competence to those seated in judgement over her. Her killings later in life, the Dunhams and her private patients in particular, could be viewed as a means to the end of an improvement in her quality of life. Removing the demand for rent, allowing her to live in the manner to which she had become accustomed after being fostered in a wealthy home, and allowing her to move freely into a new position when she tired of the current one. To many people, this motive, while the most logical and relatable, is also the most chilling. It is most unsettling to consider the idea that a person might kill and kill again, just to make their life easier.

There can be no question that Jane Toppan did kill for these reasons. She did poison people to manipulate her situation, even poisoning herself at times for the effect that it had. But the idea that any perfectly normal and sane person might at any moment simply murder another doesn't ring true. Human society as a whole has been built to prevent this kind of action. All of civility, politeness, and civilisation in general has been designed from the very beginning to make it so that our most base desires cannot rule us. So that the power of life and death is not in the hands of the individual. It is for this reason that murder is considered to be such a dangerous a crime on a societal level, not because it happens to remove one or two people from the society, but because it sets a precedent where any problem might be resolved with violence. A precedent that could lead to the complete downfall of everything.

Yet while one can look at Jane's murders and see the practicality, even without all of the social pressure to not kill, it is insufficient to explain some of her actions. There are some that she killed for her own advantage, certainly, but there are just as many that she killed with no discernable purpose whatsoever.

This observation brings us to our second option, that Jane Toppan was killing out of revenge. Her life was off to a bad start, and the kindness that she had received from others could have just as easily been seen as charity and contempt for the low-born. She was smart enough to understand the massive disparity between the wealthy and the poor, the upper and lower classes in society, and to resent that an accident of birth had placed her among the unfortunates, rather than among those who could freely dole out kindness to those unfortunates because they had been blessed with so much. Throughout her early life, she had little power that she could exercise over the world around her, having to suffer through the consequences of what others decided for her. When she became a nurse, for the very first time she was in a position where she had some control over the circumstances of others. The majority of the patients that she treated in the prestigious hospitals where she practiced were from the wealthy upper class that she resented, and where previously they could have changed the path of her life on a whim, now she was the one that had complete control over their fate. She had the power to exact revenge on them for the luck of their birth.

With a few notable exceptions where Jane was killing out of practicality, to maneuver herself into a specific situation or position, all of her victims could be considered to have been of a higher social class than her, ranging from the various landowners to the prestigious and wealthy families that she cared for. It would seem that this campaign for revenge fully encompassed her motive.

Of course, the human mind is not so simple, and neither were Jane's murders. In the preponderance of the hundred deaths that we believe she had a hand in, killing her victims was not her primary goal. Rather, what she seemed to enjoy the most was bringing her victims to the verge of death and maintaining them there for extended periods of time. She was playing god with their lives, keeping them teetering on the precipice of death without ever fully pushing them over. She was the most powerful person in their entire universe, capable of bringing them back from the dead or snuffing them out as she saw fit, and her greatest joy seemed to be in keeping them rocking back and forth for as long as she possibly could, so that she could revel in that feeling. Following this logic, Jane's motive was power. It fed her ego to have this power over her victims. It made someone who had felt powerless for too long feel like she was a god.

But of course, any nurse might have found herself in that same position of caring for those on the verge of death, with the capability right at their fingertips for either ending or saving a life. Happily, the vast majority of them never step over the line into a full on god complex, or murder. Jane Toppan was found not guilty by reason of insanity when she finally found her way to court, and while the simple fact of her murders was definitely not enough to define her as insane in the technical sense, there can be no denying that mental health issues played into the decisions that she made. We know that her family had an extensive history of mental health problems, from her sister to her father. Her father's alcoholism and self-destructive spiral were both clearly symptomatic of some deeper issue, and the way that he chose to ignore his family in favour of pursuing his own pleasures certainly points towards some form of what has come to be known as antisocial personality disorder which encompasses traits of both sociopathy and psychopathy. It is widely believed that there is a genetic component to this disorder but even if there were no genetic component, the upbringing that Jane suffered during her formative years would have been more than sufficient to cultivate that sort of personality, not to mention the damage to the structures of her brain caused by neglect and malnutrition.

Not everyone kills out of practicality, out of revenge or to massage their own ego, because most people have a sense of empathy towards the feelings of others. With the inclusion of a degree of psychopathy to the makeup, all of the other motives that have been presented for Jane's actions begin to make more sense. Her willingness to kill people just to get them out of her way is perfectly logical to a person who doesn't believe that anyone else in the world is really a full person except them.

In terms of the worst possible combinations of traits in a person that might make up a serial killer, the one that is most commonly paired up with psychopathy to create a murderer has to be sexual sadism, and by her own accounting, Jane Toppan found a sense of arousal during her long-running torture sessions. She climbed into bed with her victims, kissing them all over as they convulsed and crept towards the point of death, and she was alleged to have achieved orgasm exclusively through murder for the majority of her life.

If you attach an electrode to a monkey's brain and give it a button that it can press to stimulate the pleasure centres of its brain, that monkey will use that button over and over until it eventually starves to death. Even if Jane recognised that killing people was wrong, or self-destructive given what the consequences of discovery would be, once she had found that button and pushed it once, her life was over. There was no question that she would keep on coming back and hitting that button again and again for the rest of her life, because without empathy for others, killing was nothing more than a source of pleasure for her.

Yet all of these theories overlook the statement that Jane herself made as to what had made her into a murderer. We might have assumed it was her terrible life, her awkward positioning between social classes, her desire for revenge and power, her desire for a comfortable life but according to her, the cause of it all was heartbreak.

At the age of sixteen, she was meant to wed a boy who moved across the country and married someone else instead. It was this that Jane Toppan pointed to as the root cause of all her future actions. She never claimed it was what broke her mind and turned her into a killer, but instead looked at it through a practical lens. She believed that if she'd had a husband, she never would have become a nurse and had the opportunity to kill. If she'd had a family of her own to raise and a man to love, she never would have found the time to do any of the things that she did, instead, she would have poured all of her time and energy into them. She believed that she might have found the physical satisfaction that killing brought her in her marital bed, and never felt the need to harm anyone. We cannot turn back the clock, unravel history and see what might have unfolded if her husband-to-be had proven faithful instead of abandoning her with nothing but an engagement ring. But there can be no denying that at the heart of Jane Toppan's pathology, there was always a well of deep sadness that seemed to drive her on.

Whether it was a profound sorrow over the loss of her birth family, sadness over the loss of her beloved foster sister to the inevitability of marriage, or the loss of her own chance at marital bliss, there was an aching void at the heart of Jane Toppan that drove her to do terrible things in the pursuit of her own happiness. A sadness so profound that it justified any terrible thing that she did in life if it might diminish that sadness for even a moment. It seems as though, throughout her entire life, there was not a single minute that passed in which Jane felt happiness without it being tempered with some sorrow, guilt or dread. So perhaps the fact that she lived a long life in the care of the state after committing her crimes cannot be viewed as a mercy compared to the hangman's noose. Perhaps her nature provided justice for all of Jolly Jane's victims. They may have been dead, but at least their suffering was over. Hers was never-ending.

A life completely devoid of true happiness is the kind of fate that you would not wish on your very worst enemy.

Want More?

Did you enjoy *Angel of Death* and want some more True Crime?

YOUR FREE BOOK IS WAITING

From bestselling author Ryan Green

There is a man who is officially classed as **"Britain's most dangerous prisoner"**

The man's name is Robert Maudsley, and his crimes earned him the nickname **"Hannibal the Cannibal"**

This free book is an exploration of his story...

"Ryan brings the horrifying details to life. I can't wait to read more by this author!"

Get a free copy of **Robert Maudsley: Hannibal the Cannibal** when you sign up to join my Reader's Group.

www.ryangreenbooks.com/free-book

Every Review Helps

If you enjoyed the book and have a moment to spare, I would really appreciate a short review on Amazon. Your help in spreading the word is gratefully received and reviews make a huge difference to helping new readers find me. Without reviewers, us self-published authors would have a hard time!

Type in your link below to be taken straight to my book review page.

US	geni.us/angelUS
UK	geni.us/angelUK
Australia	geni.us/angelAUS
Canada	geni.us/angelCA

Thank you! I can't wait to read your thoughts.

About Ryan Green

Ryan Green is a true crime author who lives in Herefordshire, England with his wife, three children, and two dogs. Outside of writing and spending time with his family, Ryan enjoys walking, reading and windsurfing.

Ryan is fascinated with History, Psychology and True Crime. In 2015, he finally started researching and writing his own work and at the end of the year, he released his first book on Britain's most notorious serial killer, Harold Shipman.

He has since written several books on lesser-known subjects, and taken the unique approach of writing from the killer's perspective. He narrates some of the most chilling scenes you'll encounter in the True Crime genre.

You can sign up to Ryan's newsletter to receive a free book, updates, and the latest releases at:

WWW.RYANGREENBOOKS.COM

More Books by Ryan Green

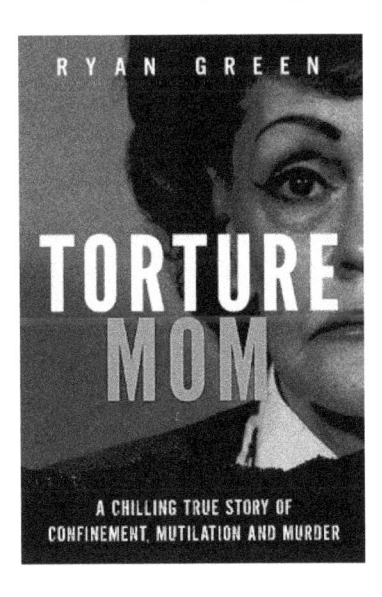

In July 1965, teenagers Sylvia and Jenny Likens were left in the temporary care of Gertrude Baniszewski, a middle-aged single mother and her seven children.

The Baniszewski household was overrun with children. There were few rules and ample freedom. Sadly, the environment created a dangerous hierarchy of social Darwinism where the strong preyed on the weak.

What transpired in the following three months was both riveting and chilling. The case shocked the entire nation and would later be described as "The single worst crime perpetuated against an individual in Indiana's history".

More Books by Ryan Green

On 29th February 2000, John Price took out a restraining order against his girlfriend, Katherine Knight. Later that day, he told his co-workers that she had stabbed him and if he were ever to go missing, it was because Knight had killed him.

The next day, Price didn't show up for work.

A co-worker was sent to check on him. They found a bloody handprint by the front door and they immediately contacted the police. The local police force was not prepared for the chilling scene they were about to encounter.

Price's body was found in a chair, legs crossed, with a bottle of lemonade under his arm. He'd been decapitated and skinned. The "skin-suit" was hanging from a meat hook in the living room and his head was found in the kitchen, in a pot of vegetables that was still warm. There were two plates on the dining table, each had the name of one of Price's children on it. She was attempting to serve his body parts to his children.

More Books by Ryan Green

In 1944, as the Nazis occupied Paris, the French Police and Fire Brigade were called to investigate a vile-smelling smoke pouring out from a Parisian home. Inside, they were confronted with a scene from a nightmare. They found a factory line of bodies and multiple furnaces stocked with human remains.

When questioned, Dr. Petiot claimed that he was a part of the Resistance and the bodies they discovered belonged to Nazi collaborators that he killed for the cause. The French Police, resentful of Nazi occupation and confused by a rational alternative, allowed him to leave.

Was the respected Doctor a clandestine hero fighting for national liberty or a deviant using dire domestic circumstances to his advantage? One thing is for certain, the Police and the Nazis both wanted to get their hands on Dr. Marcel Petiot to find out the truth.

More Books by Ryan Green

In 1861, the police of a rural French village tore their way into the woodside home of Martin Dumollard. Inside, they found chaos. Paths had been carved through mounds of bloodstained clothing, reaching as high as the ceiling in some places.

The officers assumed that the mysterious maid-robber had killed one woman but failed in his other attempts. Yet, it was becoming sickeningly clear that there was a vast gulf between the crimes they were aware of and the ones that had truly been committed.

Would Dumollard's wife expose his dark secret or was she inextricably linked to the atrocities? Whatever the circumstances, everyone was desperate to discover whether the bloody garments belonged to some of the 648 missing women.

DISCOVER MORE FROM RYAN GREEN

Stay in the loop with the latest releases and exclusive offers by following Ryan!

Follow me:

Facebook   geni.us/ryangreenFB

Instagram   geni.us/ryangreenIG

Amazon   geni.us/ryangreenAM

www.ryangreenbooks.com

RYAN GREEN

Free True Crime Audiobook

Sign up to Audible and use your free credit to download this collection of twelve books. If you cancel within 30 days, there's no charge!

WWW.RYANGREENBOOKS.COM/FREE-AUDIOBOOK

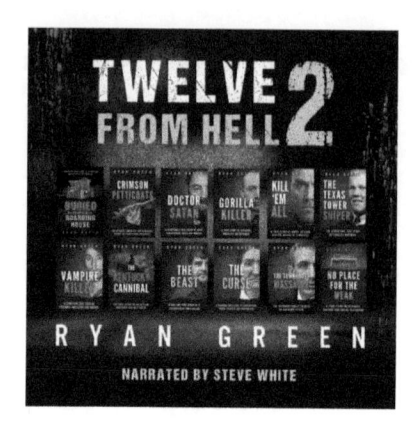

"Ryan Green has produced another excellent book and belongs at the top with true crime writers such as M. William Phelps, Gregg Olsen and Ann Rule" –**B.S. Reid**

"Wow! Chilling, shocking and totally riveting! I'm not going to sleep well after listening to this but the narration was fantastic. Crazy story but highly recommend for any true crime lover!" –**Mandy**

"Torture Mom by Ryan Green left me pretty speechless. The fact that it's a true story is just...wow" –**JStep**

"Graphic, upsetting, but superbly read and written" –**Ray C**

WWW.RYANGREENBOOKS.COM/FREE-AUDIOBOOK